HENRY V

ye and noble prince excellent
My lord the prince, my lord gracious
I humble servant and obedient
unto yowr estate hye and glorious

HENRY V

The rebirth of chivalry

MALCOLM MERCER

THE NATIONAL ARCHIVES

First published in 2004 by

The National Archives
Kew, Richmond
Surrey TW9 4DU
UK

www.nationalarchives.gov.uk/

The National Archives (TNA) was formed when the Public Record Office and
Historical Manuscripts Commission (HMC) combined in April 2003

ISBN 1 903365 71 6

Designed by Penny Jones and Michael Morris, Brentford, Middlesex

Printed in the UK by Butler and Tanner Ltd, Frome, Somerset

ILLUSTRATIONS

Cover: Portrait of Henry V (detail), artist unknown; confirmation of treaty between
Henry V and Sigismund, Emperor-Elect of the Holy Roman Empire, 1416;
(background) account of costs and expenses from the Agincourt campaign, 1415–16.

Half-title page: A miniature watercolour of Henry V painted on vellum by the artist,
Bernard Lens (III, the younger) dated 1732. The portrait shows a youthful monarch
with a sword resting on his right shoulder, the hallmark of a medieval warrior-king.

Frontispiece: Henry V as a patron of learning. The King, standing on the right, is being
offered a book, *The Regement of Princes*, by its author Thomas Hoccleve. Hoccleve's
book was completed in 1411 and continued the tradition of Lancastrian patronage for
works of political advice. It remained popular throughout the fifteenth century.

Title page: Henry V's Great Seal. This impression of the reverse shows the King on
horseback. The seal appears on a grant dated 26 October 1414 confirming previous
grants by Henry IV, Richard II, Edward III and Henry III to the Abbot and Convent of
St Edward.

Contents page: Scene from the battle of Agincourt (detail), 25 October 1415, copied
by a nineteenth-century artist from an original medieval depiction.

Page x (facing Preface): Seals of Henry V. Dominating this engraving are the obverse
and reverse faces of the Great Seal of Henry V. The design of the Great Seal follows
the standard pattern with representations of the King sitting in state (obverse), and
on horseback (reverse). However, Henry was the first king of England to adopt the
new-style arms of France with three fleur-de-lys on his seal as well as placing England
before France on the legend. On the bottom left is the seal of Queen Katharine; on
the right is the seal of Henry as Prince of Wales.

Contents

Acknowledgements

I would like to thank the many people who have helped in the production of this book, not least through their encouragement, advice and support:

Rosemary Amos, Jim Bolton, Jane Crompton, Sean Cunningham, Keith Dockray, Peter Fleming, David Grummitt, Agnieszka Jarecka, Michael K Jones, Hannes Kleineke, Clive Mercer, Elizabeth Morrison, Jenny Speller and James Travers.

In particular I owe a big debt of gratitude to Stephen O'Connor for his guidance and assistance with the document translations.

This book is dedicated to my parents, Patricia and David, for helping me to achieve my dreams.

Series Note

Most of the key historic documents selected for this series are from the collections at The National Archives; a few are reproduced courtesy of other important national or private repositories.

Each key document is reproduced on a numbered double-page spread with an explanatory introduction placing it in context. (Selected pages or details have been chosen for lengthy items.) Transcripts, with modernized spellings and explanations of archaic words, are provided where necessary. All the documents featured on these spreads are cross-referenced in the main text.

If you would like to see the original documents at The National Archives at Kew, please see www.nationalarchives.gov.uk or phone 020 8392 5200 for information about how to obtain a free Reader's Ticket.

For further information about titles in the ENGLISH MONARCHS series or other publications from The National Archives, please send your name and address to:

Publications Marketing, FREEPOST SEA 7565, Richmond, Surrey, UK TW9 4DU (stamp required from overseas)

To order any publication from The National Archives, visit www.nationalarchives.gov.uk/bookshop/

The Documents

Preface

It is unlikely that many people would claim never to have heard of Henry V or his military successes against the French. Whilst other medieval monarchs won significant victories against the 'ancient enemy' across the Channel, it was those of Henry V which remained in the public consciousness more than any others. Chief amongst these, of course, was Agincourt. It was on 25 October 1415, the Feast of Saints Crispin and Crispinian, that an English army numbering no more than 6,000 men and commanded by its warrior-king, overcame a far superior French army numbering about 20,000.

Hailed by contemporary chroniclers as the flower of English chivalry, few English monarchs drew as much military prestige to the Crown as Henry V. In a reign which lasted no more than nine-and-a-half years, this second king of the Lancastrian dynasty placed England firmly on the European landscape. The reverses to national pride which had been inflicted upon England under Richard II and Henry IV were consigned firmly to the past. Moreover, it was these victories that succeeding generations of kings of England sought to evoke when undertaking their own enterprises in continental Europe.

The sources for Henry's life have received considerable attention from generations of historians. Indeed, from the very moment of his death, chroniclers were recording his deeds for future generations to marvel at. It is not realistic to compete against such stiff competition. To a large degree, the Henry V that the public recognizes is the Henry presented by Shakespeare. Although not vilified, as Richard III was by the Bard, Henry's career did not escape unscathed. The events of his life were manipulated to suit the points which Shakespeare wished to present to his audience. This book seeks to move away from the Shakespearean Henry and instead to set him within a contemporary context, using a selection of key sources from The National Archives in their original form.

Troubled Times:
The Childhood and Youth
of Henry Monmouth

A FUTURE KING IS BORN

When a baby boy was born in a rather dilapidated chamber of the gatehouse tower of Monmouth Castle sometime in August or September 1386 it went largely unnoticed. The baby, christened Henry, was the first son of Henry Bolingbroke, Earl of Derby and his wife, Mary de Bohun. Bolingbroke was the eldest son of England's premier nobleman, John of Gaunt, Duke of Lancaster, third son of Edward III. Mary was the second daughter of the powerful magnate, Humphrey, Earl of Hereford, Essex and Northampton and a rich heiress in her own right. Although his prestigious ancestry marked the young Henry out as somebody who could expect to become a leading noblemen once he reached adulthood, there was little else about his birth to attract attention. Read the only evidence of Henry's birth: document 1, *Henry of Monmouth*.

Portrait of Richard II. This wood panel painting was probably commissioned in the mid-1390s. Richard is shown seated in state, regally and frontally, crowned and holding a sceptre and orb, the symbols of royal authority. Richard's aggressive promotion of his regal state was to lead to conflict with his subjects and ultimately to his deposition.

Historians know relatively little about Henry of Monmouth's childhood. He certainly had a nurse, Joan Waryn, for whom he retained a great deal of affection throughout his life. Henry and his brothers and sisters no doubt spent their earliest years in her company. Between 1390 and 1394, however, his father spent a lot of time away from England, crusading against the pagan Lithuanians in Eastern Europe. During his absence, and especially after the death of Mary de Bohun in 1394, Henry and his siblings were

1 *Henry of Monmouth*

There is virtually no surviving evidence about the birth of Henry V, apart from a stray reference relating to the event in the gatehouse tower of Monmouth Castle almost 60 years later, in a warrant dated 12 February 1445. It is only because this warrant was subsequently enrolled on a Duchy of Lancaster Chancery Roll that historians have been able to determine this crucial fact.

Henry of Monmouth had never been expected to succeed to the throne when he was born, probably in September 1386. Richard II was King and still had every chance of producing a male heir during his lifetime. As far as the world at large was concerned, Henry was simply the first-born son of one of England's premier noblemen, Henry Bolingbroke, Earl of Derby. Bolingbroke was the heir of John of Gaunt, Duke of Lancaster and was thus first cousin of the King. As such, the young Henry of Monmouth was destined for a role as one of England's leading magnates.

Monmouth Castle had been built on a strategic position, guarding crossings of the rivers Wye and Monnow. It was therefore important that its defensive readiness was maintained. Unfortunately, it was not uncommon for castles to fall into ruin in the late Middle Ages. Periodically orders were given to royal officials to make repairs. The funding might come from the Exchequer but not exclusively so. The Duchy of Lancaster was the private domain of the kings of England and the necessary resources would be expected to come from the Duchy in the first instance. Here, Henry Coly of Monmouth was authorized to receive the goods and chattels of felons, the money from the sale of wood in the locality, and other miscellaneous profits of the Lordship of Monmouth to finance the work.

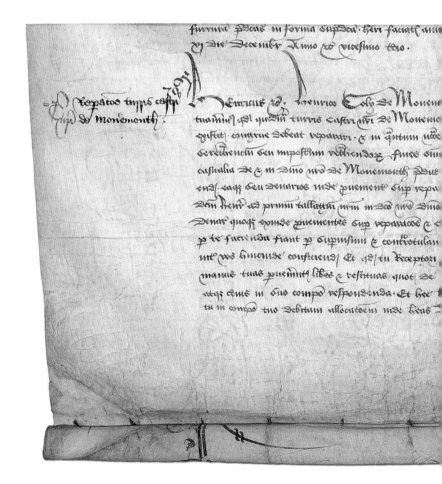

THE WARRANT READS:

Henry, etc, to Henry Coly of Monmouth, greetings. Whereas we, by the advice of the Council of our Duchy of Lancaster, have appointed and agreed that a certain tower of our Castle of Monmouth, where our dear Prince of celebrated memory [Henry V] was born, called 'the gatehouse', which exists in a much wasted and ruined state, needs to be suitably repaired and to be built anew in so far as would be necessary. Know that we have assigned you, the aforesaid, the goods and chattels of customary tenants or future re-sales, fines of all felons, and incoming money from the sale of wood from Bukholt and also all other incidental profits of and in our aforesaid Lordship of Monmouth.

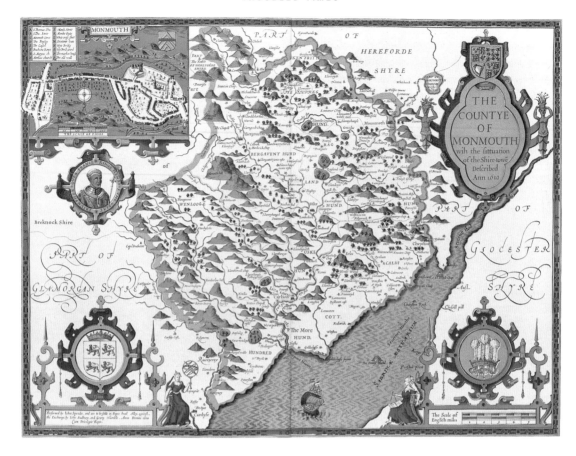

Early seventeenth-century engraving of the county of Monmouth taken from John Speed's *Theatre of the Empire of Great Britain* published in 1610. Inset in the top left-hand corner is a small plan showing the town and castle of Monmouth where Henry V was born in 1386.

placed in the care of their maternal grandmother, Joan, Countess of Hereford, who lived at Bytham in Lincolnshire under the day-to-day supervision of a governess called Mary Hervy.

Henry's upbringing and education would have followed that of any young nobleman of the time. He would first have studied Latin grammar before moving on to chronicles, romances and other works of literature. However, the influence of his father, who also possessed a keen interest in literature and the arts, meant that his education was probably much more rigorous than that of his contemporaries. A love of literature and the arts was to remain with Henry throughout his life. It seems likely that he also developed a passion for music and it has been suggested that he learned to play the harp as a boy.

As the son of a major nobleman, though, Henry's education would have focused increasingly on more traditional noble pursuits. He would have learned to ride, hunt and, most importantly, to fight. It is very likely that from his earliest years, Henry was developing a keen interest in chivalry, not least from the example presented by his father on crusade who was publicly demonstrating his military prowess for a righteous cause.

AN UNCERTAIN FUTURE

Henry's formative years should also be set within the context of England's troubled domestic political scene. The revolution of 1399 catapulted the House of Lancaster to the forefront of English politics and in the process fundamentally altered Henry of Monmouth's future. From 1396 onwards the King, Richard II, acted in an increasingly autocratic manner towards his subjects, especially the nobility. Rather than rely on the advice and counsel of the traditional nobility Richard had preferred to listen to his favourites to whom he also granted peerages.

In 1398 England was plunged into turmoil after the King sentenced Henry's father, the recently created Duke of Hereford, to exile. Hereford's exile had been brought about by a casual conversation that he had with Thomas Mowbray, Duke of Norfolk, who had remarked to him that the King was determined to bring about their downfall. Hereford had repeated this to his father, Gaunt, who had then informed the King.

Engraving showing the elaborate canopied tomb of John of Gaunt, Duke of Lancaster and his third wife, Katherine Swynford. Gaunt was buried in St Paul's Cathedral in a tomb which was later destroyed by the Great Fire of 1666. Gaunt played a major role in the politics of England for much of Richard II's reign. It was the seizure of the Duchy of Lancaster on Gaunt's death in 1399 which resulted in the establishment of the Lancastrian dynasty.

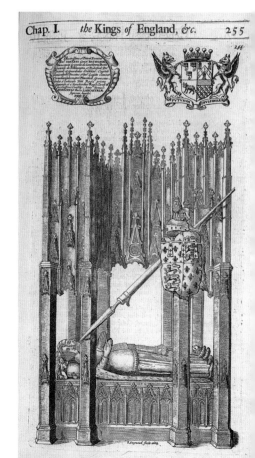

7

Seal of John of Gaunt, Duke of Lancaster, attached to an indenture, dated 16 August 1392 leasing the manor of Daventry for 12 years to William and John. The seal quarters the royal arms of England with those of Castile to which the Duke had a claim by his second wife, Constance, daughter of Peter the Cruel, King of Castile.

As a result Hereford was forced to confront Norfolk in the presence of the King who ordered a hearing of the matter before the Court of Chivalry. The Court subsequently decided that the case should be decided through trial by combat. The encounter never took place. Instead Richard decided that Norfolk should be banished from England for life; Hereford escaped relatively lightly and was only banished for 10 years. Despite such drastic action disaster could have been averted after Hereford and Gaunt accepted the King's decision. Yet Richard then went one stage further by confiscating the estates of the Duchy of Lancaster when Gaunt died on 3 February 1399. This sent a very clear message across society: a man's lands were not safe from such a despotic monarch.

Scene from Jean Creton's *Histoire du Roy d'Angleterre* depicting the knighting of Henry of Monmouth (left-hand corner) by Richard II during the royal expedition to Ireland in 1399. Although treated honourably by the King, Henry was imprisoned by Richard in the castle of Trim before returning to England.

The consequences of Richard's actions went much deeper than the defence of property. The King still had no heir to succeed him. To some sections of the nobility, Hereford's claim to the throne as a descendant of Edward III was a strong one. As confidence in Richard continued to diminish, the opposition to him started to take shape. In the spring of 1399 the King was forced to go on campaign in Ireland to quell a rebellion by Art MacMurrough, King of Leinster. With him he took the 12-year-old Henry of Monmouth. During the campaign he was knighted by the King and treated with due respect and honour, something which he was to remember in later life when he reburied Richard II's body in Westminster Abbey in 1413. Yet Henry's presence in Ireland was undoubtedly a reflection of the King's concern that Hereford might pose a threat to his rule in the near future.

TRIUMPH OF THE HOUSE OF LANCASTER

In fact, Hereford possessed precisely those qualities which many looked for in a king. He was a distinguished soldier, experienced politician, conventionally pious, and a highly cultured and literate man. In attempting a political comeback in 1399 it is unclear whether he was deliberately aiming for the throne. Nevertheless, early in July Hereford landed with a small force of about 300 men at Ravenspur in the East Riding of Yorkshire. He claimed to have returned to recover his inheritance.

Richard was still in Ireland but seemed uncertain how to respond. When he heard the news he subsequently called Henry into his presence and told him his father's actions would cost him his inheritance. Henry is said to have replied that he had known

Flint Castle where Richard II finally surrendered himself to his cousin, Henry Bolingbroke in August 1399. Deserted by all but his closest companions, Richard had no choice other than to seek to come to terms with his captor. Once in Bolingbroke's hands though, the King's fate was sealed.

Scene from Jean Creton's *Histoire du Roy d'Angleterre* showing Richard II led captive to London by Henry Bolingbroke where he abdicates in favour of Henry. The official version of events naturally records that Richard did this willingly, but an eye-witness account states he resisted for some time before agreeing to become Sir Richard of Bordeaux, a mere knight.

nothing of his father's plans. Probably as a form of insurance policy, Richard incarcerated Henry in the castle of Trim to the north-west of Dublin before returning to his Kingdom across the Irish Sea. He landed in South Wales but when he discovered that his nobles were starting to desert him, he then marched northwards to Conway Castle. He quickly entered into communication with Hereford who was by this time based at Chester. Hereford invited the King to restore his Lancastrian inheritance and attend a meeting of Parliament. As soon as he left the castle, however, he was ambushed by one of Hereford's supporters, Henry Percy, Earl of Northumberland, and taken to meet him at Flint Castle.

Hereford, now styling himself Duke of Lancaster, had become effective ruler of England. Summons to a Parliament were quickly sent out in the King's name. In the meantime Richard was taken from Chester down to London where he was lodged in the Tower. At about the same time Henry was brought over from Ireland and reunited with his father. According to pro-Lancastrian accounts Richard was asked to abdicate in favour of the new Duke of Lancaster by a special committee of churchmen, nobles and lawyers on 29 September 1399. He supposedly did this willingly. Lancaster ascended the throne as Henry IV. There was some uncertainty as to how he could justify his title to the throne given the circumstances in which he had come to power. Eventually it was decided to base his claim on his undisputed descent from Henry III, the will of God, and Richard II's responsibility for the failure of good government in the Kingdom. Learn more about a key supporter of the House of Lancaster: document 2, *The coronation of Henry IV*.

An illuminated initial 'H' from The Great Cowcher containing a miniature of Henry IV, the first king of the Lancastrian dynasty. The Great Cowcher, or *Carte Regum*, was a large register containing copies of deeds and other documents relating to the Duchy of Lancaster's possessions in England and Wales. It is in two volumes and contains 2,400 deeds. Begun in 1402 by John Leventhorpe, Receiver of the Duchy, on the orders of Henry IV, it was apparently an attempt to centralize information from the Duchy's record repositories.

2 The coronation of Henry IV

A petition from Henry Percy, Earl of Northumberland to perform service at the coronation ceremony, 1399.

A significant factor in the success of Henry Bolingbroke in 1399 was the support of the Percy family. The Percys held extensive estates in Northumberland, Cumberland and Yorkshire and were the most powerful magnate family on the Scottish border. Henry, Lord Percy was created Earl of Northumberland in 1377 at Richard II's coronation. During his reign, Northumberland's authority in the north had been enhanced by his appointment to the Wardenships of the East and West Marches. The Earl exercised a moderating role in national politics. He advised the King to negotiate with the Lords Appellant in 1387 and intervened on behalf of the

Duke of Gloucester and Richard FitzAlan, Earl of Arundel before the Royal Council in 1389.

Despite the Earl's moderate stance, Richard II removed the Percys from their Wardenships in 1396. It is possible that this high-handed treatment alienated them and prompted them to back Henry Boling-broke's coup in 1399. The Percys played a prominent part in the coronation of the new King. On that day Northumberland carried the first sword at the left shoulder of the King. In his petition, the penultimate entry of this document, Northumberland stated that the King had granted him that right – to carry 'Lancaster's Sword' – when he had landed at Holderness (in Humberside).

The newly crowned Henry IV, first

King of the Lancastrian dynasty, restored the family to its prominent position on the border. Northumberland was reappointed to his Wardenships. Moreover, in 1402, Northumberland and his son, Henry Percy, known as 'Hotspur', defeated the Scots at Homildon Hill. As a reward he was given the Earldom of Douglas. However, he had first to conquer it at his own expense. The Percy family was also given a dominant role in north Wales and Cheshire. It was from here that Northumberland's son 'Hotspur' launched his rebellion against Henry IV in 1403. Northumberland was acquitted for his involvement but rebelled again in 1405 for which he was convicted. He rebelled yet again in 1408 but was defeated by the sheriff of Yorkshire at Bramham Moor in 1408.

THE PETITION READS:

Likewise, the same Henry of Percy, Earl of Northumberland and Constable of England, by personally appearing in the aforesaid court, asserted and alleged that our aforesaid Lord King himself willed and granted that the same Earl, in return for the gift of the Isle of Man, the same island having been granted to him and his heirs by the Lord King and his heirs, should have and hold the same island by service of carrying on the day of the coronation of the said King and his heirs on the left shoulder of the same King and on the left shoulder of his heir, by himself or by his sufficient and honourable deputy, that naked sword which the aforesaid King wore called 'Lancaster's Sword', by which the aforesaid King had been girded when he landed in the parts of Holderness as Duke of Lancaster before his coronation, during the procession and at all times during the ceremony of the aforesaid coronation. He petitions that he be permitted to perform at the aforesaid service on the day of the aforesaid coronation according to that which is wished and appointed. And because the aforesaid court has agreed that what the Earl has alleged is true, the aforesaid Earl was permitted to perform that service which he performed personally on the day of the aforesaid coronation.

In parliamento ad Westm' Dñi Regis Henrici secundi post conquestum Anno Dñi mill'mo tricen'mo vicesimo nono Anno vero Regni ipsius Regis vicesimo tercio apud Westm' convocato Anno die mensis Septembris cessione et resignacione eiusdem Regis prelatis proceribus et Communitati totius regni publice notificatis ab eisdem admissis Ac ipso Rege propter sua demerita deposito Successit eidem Henricus dux Lancastrie comes Derb' Lincoln' Leycestr' herefordie et Northampton Seneschallus Anglie Et cum tractaretur et provisum fuisset de solempni coronacione ipsius regis Henrici die Lune in festo translacionis sancti Edwardi Regis et confessoris tunc vix sequenti celebrand' dictus dñus noster Rex ut in iure comitatus sui Leycestrie cui officium Seneschalli pertinet idem officium comisit Thome filio suo in coronacione predicta faciend' quod quidem officium idem Thomas tam in propria persona sua quam in persona dñi Thome de Percy Comitis Wygorn' qui pater eum ministravit predictus Thome filii regis eidem assignatus erat in auxilium predictum officium exercuit de precepto predicti Regis Henrici et feode eidem officio consueta clamabit et precepit in coronacione prefati dñi Henrici die Lune apud Westm' solempniter facta et celebrata.

Et memorandum quod prefatus Thomas filius Regis die Sabbati videlicet quarto die Octobris ante coronacionem predictam sedebat de precepto Regis tanquam Seneschallus Anglie in alba aula regis palacii Westm' pro capellam regulam et inquirebat diligenter que et qualia officia seu feoda dicto die de gnostmeis faciend' vel optinend' fuerunt et cum hoc eodem publice proclamari fecit quod omni magnates et alii qui aliqua officia ad coronacionem predictam facere seu aliqua feoda optinere clamare vellent billas et peticiones suas clamea sua continentes coram ipso Seneschallo vel eius in hac parte deputato proferri facerent nobilite Et super quo diversa officia et feoda tam per peticiones qui oretenus coram ipso Seneschallo exorta et benedicta exorterunt in forma que subsequitur.

In primis Henricus primogenitus predicti Regis Henrici quem ipse Rex ut in iure ducatus sui Lancastrie assignabat ad gerendum principalem gladium primo ante Regem vocatum Curtana die coronacionis eiusdem Regis officium illud fuit ex huiusmodi assignacione clamabit et in propria persona decenter ibidem exercuit et gessit.

Item Johannes comes Somers' cui predictus Rex Henricus ut in iure Comitatus sui Lincoln' officium assignaverit ad standendum et secund' coram eo sedentem ad mensam dicto die coronacionis sue officium illud facere ex huiusmodi assignacione clamabat et sic fecit in propria persona.

Item quo ad officium Constabul' Anglie Henricus comes Northumbr' cui predictus Rex officium constabul' Anglie concesserat ut asserit ipse comes habend' ad terminum vite sue officium illud facere et feoda eidem consueta papere clamabit virtute concessionis predicte et quia nullus huius clameo contradixit ideo consideratum fuit quod de voluntate dni Regis predictus comes ad predictum officium admitteretur et ita ipse comes officium illud in omnibus postmodum adimplevit feoda eidem officio consueta papiendo.

Item idem Henricus de Percy comes Northumbr' et constabularius Anglie in Curia predicta personaliter comparens asseruit et allegavit quod predictus dñus noster Rex voluit et ipsi assignavit quod idem comes pro insula de Man sibi et heredibus suis per prefatum dñum Regem concessa eandem insulam de dicto dño Rege de Sabbati die habend' et teneret per servicium portandi sibi coronacione dicti Regis cum cedanum suorum ad sinistrum humerum ipsius Regis et ad sinistros humeros heredum suarum per seipsum aut sufficientem et honorificam deputatum suum illum gladium in dño quo cinctus erat prefatus Rex quando ipse ante coronacionem suam vero de dño Lancastrie in partibus de Holdernesse applicuit vocatum lancastre swerd Durante processione et toto tempore solempnizacionis coronacionis predicte Petendo se ad servicium predictum die coronacionis predicte mota solennitatem et assignacionem predictas admitti Et quia Curie predicte satis constabat premissa per prefatum comitem sic allegata verritatem continere Ideo comes admissus fuit ad servicium predictum faciend' quod quidem servicium idem comes in die coronacionis predicte personaliter faciebat.

Item quo ad officium Mareschalli Anglie Radulphus comes Westmerland cui predictus Rex officium mareschalli Anglie concesserat ut asserit ipse comes habend' ad terminum vite sue officium illud facere et feoda eidem consueta papere clamabit virtute concessionis predicte Recepundus Burgh Robertus Consill' et Thomas Brinham asserentes se attornatos Thome Ducis Norff' perveverunt quandam supplicacionem in hec verba A mō treshonouree le Seneschal dengleterre Supplient les attornes leur treshonouree Thomas Duc de Norff' Mareschal dengleterre que come il en soit enherite a luy et a ses heires nusles de son corps engendrez par titre de souffisaunt et de mesme loffice ovec les fees prouffitz et toutes autres choses a icel office appurtenantz ou regardantz en pleine seisine et possession estoit Que plaise a vie honour de considerer que le dit Duc est bonde; hors du Roialme par iuggement et ordeinance del Roy Richard qui darein estoit fait a Couentree et est es parties loing terres a luy assignees par mesme lordeinance sanz avoir notice de la coronacion nostre tresredoubte seignur le Roy here est et a le dit Duc par iuggement vers luy nient sune nun sive nummere nub forfait le dit office nienment puplies de sa enheritance en succession Accepter et par tant y assigner aucune souffisante psonme des attornes du dit Duc pour sure exer et continuer le dit office et ppning du dit office appert pour son nom et lestat du dit Duc et les fees et prouffitz au dit office apppenantz ou regardantz preudre aucun receiure a enoier en nom a dror Norff' lheir treshonouree le Duc avandit Cui quo in tu peticione predicta dictum fuit pro dicto dño Rege quod officium illud in persona ipsius dñi Regis in feod' remansit ad assignandum et concedendum cuicumque sibi placeret Ad quod nichil allegaverunt erat et ideo prefatus comes Westmerland assignatus fuit ad officium predictum faciend' papiendo feoda debita et consueta Et sic idem Radulphus officium illud presens et feoda debita et consueta hac vice precepit Salvis vero quibuscumque eum inde loqui voluerunt.

Here shewes howe at the batell of Shrewesbury, betwen kyng Henry the
iiijth & Sr Henry Percy / Erle Richard there beyng on the kynge party ful
notably & manly behaved hym self, to his grete lawde & Worship. In
which batell was slayne the said Sr Henry Percy and many other wt
hym. And on the kyng party there was slayne in the kyng co te wyt
chef of other, the Erle of Stafford, Erle Richardes Awnter son wt
many other in grete noumbre. on Whoes Sowles god have mcy Amen

Developing a Taste for Power: Henry, Prince of Wales and the Government of England

SECURING THE DYNASTY

The battle of Shrewsbury, 21 July 1403, taken from the *Beauchamp Pageant*, a manuscript possibly produced in Bruges in the late fifteenth century. The forces of Henry IV are on the left of the picture, with Richard Beauchamp, Earl of Warwick in the centre. Immediately opposite him is Henry Percy, known as 'Hotspur', falling back-wards after having been pierced through the breast by an arrow. In the fore-ground a footsoldier with a spear stands over a fallen archer.

A heavy gold Noble of Henry IV. On the obverse the King is armed in a ship, and the heraldic arms on the shield show the three leopards of England in two of the quarters and the old arms with four fleur-de-lys of France in the other two quarters.

It is only with the coronation of his father as Henry IV on 13 October 1399 that Henry of Monmouth finally steps into the limelight. On 15 October Parliament agreed that he should be created Prince of Wales, Duke of Cornwall and Earl of Chester, the titles traditionally conferred upon a king's eldest son. On 16 October it was decided that he should also be granted the title of Duke of Aquitaine. Finally, on 10 November, the King proposed that the Duchy of Lancaster should be conferred upon Henry. Significantly, however, it was to be held separately by his heirs from the Crown of England. Future kings of England would henceforth also be private landowners in their own right.

Despite the pomp and ceremony of the coronation, the House of Lancaster was by no means secure. Rumours of the survival of Richard II, thought to have been starved to death in Pontefract Castle early in 1400, continued to haunt Henry IV for a number of years. The first serious challenge came when rebellion broke out in Wales in 1400. Henry, Prince of Wales was only 14 years old. Yet he was soon called upon

to play an active role defending his family's title to the Crown. The Principality was to dominate his attention for the next 10 years. It was during these formative years that the Prince acquired his education in the art of warfare.

The landscape of North Wales. It was in this rugged terrain that Glyndwr raised his rebellion against Henry IV and declared himself Prince of Wales. North Wales was ideally suited to Glyndwr's campaign of guerrilla warfare and it was not until 1409 that the English were able effectively to crush the rebellion.

It appears that unrest in Wales stemmed from a local dispute between Reginald, Lord Grey of Ruthin and one of his neighbours, Owain Glyndwr. It had rapidly escalated though on 16 September 1400 when Glyndwr, a descendant of Welsh princes, had declared himself Prince of Wales. In quick succession he attacked Ruthin, Denbigh and other places in Flintshire, before moving southwards to assault Oswestry and Welshpool. Although the rebels were halted by an English force led by Hugh, Lord Burnell, the rebellion quickly adopted a nationalist flavour which aimed at ending English rule in Wales.

Owain Glyndwr's Armorial Mount found at Harlech Castle in 1923. It shows the arms of the princes of Gwynedd which he adopted. Coming from a native Welsh family, Glyndwr could claim descent from all three of the major royal houses that had dominated Wales prior to the Edwardian conquest of 1282. The quartered shield bears lions rampant, corresponding to those of Glyndwr as Prince of Wales.

The Prince moved up to Chester soon after news of the rebellion reached him, along with his governor, Sir Hugh Despenser and his principal adviser, Henry Percy, son of the Earl of Northumberland, known as 'Hotspur'. To those at Court it looked as if the rebellion would end as quickly as it had begun. However, the daring capture of Conway Castle by Gwilym and Rhys ap Tudor on Good Friday, 1 April 1401, rekindled Welsh resistance to the English. Despite the Prince's attempt to recapture Conway, and campaigns by Percy in Merionethshire and Lord Powys in central Wales, the rebellion gained momentum. It continued into 1402 with no indication that English efforts to crush it were having any success. Read about Prince Henry's activities in Wales: document 3, *Glyndwr's rebellion*.

The Prince gradually assumed control of operations against the Welsh. Whilst experienced commanders like the Earls of Arundel and Stafford, Lord Grey of Codnor and Lord Powys were given particular areas of responsibility in Wales and on the border with England, they were placed firmly under the Prince's command. In 1403 his authority was enhanced further when he was appointed Royal Lieutenant for the whole of Wales for a year, a significant step in his military and political education.

The Great Seal of Owain Glyndwr. It only survives in a single impression attached to his 1404 treaty with Charles VI of France. It is of very fine workmanship and was possibly commissioned in France. On the obverse, Owain is shown enthroned beneath a canopy of state, holding a sceptre, but with no crown. A lawyer by training, here he represents the role of a king as the giver of justice. As in French royal seals, angels hold up his cloth of majesty, which shows the lions rampant of Gwynedd. His feet rest on two more lions, and two wolf heads spring from the arms of his throne. On the reverse, Owain appears on horseback as the warrior and feudal leader he also was – this time with a crown on his helmet. The Welsh dragon appears on both his helmet, and on the warhorse's head. The legend is now incomplete, but by putting the two sides together probably read OWYNUS DEI GRATIA PRINCEPS WALLIAE – 'Owain, by the grace of God, Prince of Wales'.

A warrant authorizing payment to Prince Henry to crush the rebels in Wales, 30 August 1401.

As Prince of Wales, Henry was nominally in command of royal forces sent to crush Owain Glyndwr's rebellion the moment it broke out in 1401. Royal commands were addressed to the Prince in the first instance, even though it was down to his lieutenants and officers actually to execute them.

From 1403 Prince Henry assumed a more prominent role in directing operations. The Wales that he had to deal with was not, however, the tribal Wales of popular imagination. Before and after the conquest by Edward I in the thirteenth century a new class of gentry had been developing. In certain areas large integrated individual estates had displaced the system of semi-communal land-holding by a group of relatives. This shift away from tribalism to a move to a more feudal structure of landholding had in part been brought about by a closer association with England. It had been reinforced by growth of local administrative institutions and the need for individuals to staff offices within it. Amongst those who had benefited from this process were Glyndwr and his kinsmen, the Tudors.

Glyndwr was one of the few Welsh landowners who held lands directly from the Crown which their ancestors had ruled as princes. The early career of Glyndwr also makes it apparent that the Welshmen opposed to Prince Henry were not wild tribesmen. He had been 'an apprentice-at-law', probably at the Inns of Court in Westminster, had participated in the Scottish expedition of 1385, and whilst at Berwick was described by one Welsh chronicler as 'wearing in his helmet the scarlet feather of a flamingo'. He was of sufficient status even to give evidence in the famous Scrope versus Grosvenor case heard before the Court of Chivalry. Glyndwr and his principal followers were men who understood English government, law and methods of warfare. It was this knowledge that made them so difficult to defeat.

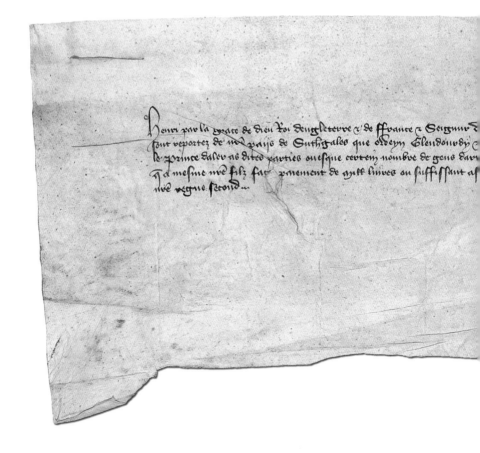

THE WARRANT READS:

Henry, by the grace of God, King of England and of France and Lord of Ireland. To the Treasurer and Chamberlains of our Exchequer greetings. Forasmuch as [since] certain news recently reported to us from our country of South Wales that Owain Glyn Dwr and others of our rebels there have risen against us and our Majesty, we have ordered our very dear son, the Prince to go to the said parts with a certain number of men-at-arms and archers in his company to resist the malice of our said rebels. We therefore order you to pay the same Prince £1,000 or sufficient assignment [amount] for the said cause above. Given under our Privy Seal at Westminster the 30th day of August in the 2nd year of our reign.

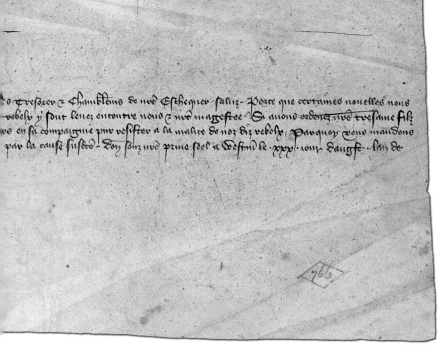

Prince Henry's appointment was part of an attempt to fill the vacuum of authority and loyalty that had become prevalent in the Principality. Indentures of service which were signed by captains with the Prince stressed the fact that they were serving him. The Prince's growing role was reflected further in his appointment of lieutenants to act for him in his Earldom of Chester. His constant presence was required in Wales and he frequently found himself travelling the length and breadth of the border directing operations and co-ordinating the English responses to Welsh incursions.

Portrait of Sir Henry Percy. The eldest son of Henry Percy, 1st Earl of Northumberland, he was nicknamed 'Hotspur' by his Scottish enemies in recognition of his martial talents. Embittered by the lack of favour shown by Henry IV towards the Percys, father and son rebelled against the King. However, Hotspur was intercepted near Shrewsbury by Henry IV on 21 July 1403 before he could join forces with his father, and was killed in the battle.

THE PERCY REVOLT

In early 1403 the English switched tactics. Conducting raids against the Welsh was abandoned in favour of strengthening the garrisons of key strategic castles such as Conway and Caernarvon. However, this change in approach was overshadowed by the dramatic turn of events when the Percy family raised the standard of rebellion against Henry IV that summer. There had already been signs that the Percys were becoming disillusioned with the new regime the previous year. At Court they had been advocating a compromise with Glyndwr, a policy the King would not entertain in the slightest. As the Prince gradually assumed a more prominent role in Welsh operations, their influence in that theatre had witnessed a marked decline as well.

Percy and his uncle, the Earl of Worcester, now turned against the House of Lancaster claiming that Richard II was alive and well. In a bold move, they rushed towards Shrewsbury with their army hoping to capture the Prince and use him as a pawn against his father. Their forces included a large contingent from Cheshire and Flint. Some were their own supporters whilst others, like Sir William Stanley, had defected from the Prince's retinue. Before they could do this, though, they were brought to battle by the King. Henry IV had moved westwards from Northampton where he was joined by Prince Henry, busy recruiting for another Welsh campaign.

The battle of Shrewsbury on 21 July was a hard-fought and bloody affair. During the battle the Prince received a nasty wound in the face from an arrow but refused to retire from the conflict. Despite the superior size of the royal army, the outcome of the battle was by no means certain until 'Hotspur' was killed. Panic spread quickly through the rebel army and many were killed as they fled

Warkworth Castle was part of the chain of defensive castles built against the Scots on the northern border. In 1332 the castle came into the possession of the Percy family. The unusually shaped keep was built in 1390. It is basically a square with towers projecting on each of its four sides. The castle became a favourite residence of the Percys, but in 1405 it was besieged and taken by Henry IV when the family rebelled against the King. Subsequently restored to the family, major additions and alterations were carried out to it in the fifteenth century. The castle was kept in good repair until the mid-sixteenth century.

the battlefield. According to chronicle accounts, 36 of the King's knights and eight of Percy's knights were killed. In addition 1,847 dead were buried in a single pit on the battlefield. Many prisoners were also taken including the Earl of Worcester. Worcester and some of his leading supporters were publicly executed in Shrewsbury two days later. Learn more about the Percy rebels: document 4, *Reasons for rebelling*.

Following the defeat of the Percys, operations in Wales were resumed once more. These continued throughout 1404 with the Prince remaining intimately involved in all aspects of their planning and direction. At the beginning of January 1405 he reported to the King and his Council that the Welsh were preparing an attack on Hereford. In early March he wrote again reporting a victory won against a force of 8,000 rebels. This had been achieved very much with the support of his own Princely household which had been placed on a war-footing for a number of years. See evidence of the Prince's household mobilized for war: document 5, *'The Wages of War'*.

The report of the Prince's victory was received in London with great joy, and in Parliament he was praised as a young man of great heart and courage. By 1406 he had achieved mastery in Wales. The English continued to strengthen their grip on Wales. The extra men and money which had been poured into the Principality were now having a telling effect. Following the recapture of Harlech and Aberystwyth Castles by the English in 1409, Glyndwr's cause was doomed. He conducted one final raid across the border into Shropshire in 1410 but thereafter he disappeared completely into the mists of history. When it was eventually decided to offer him a royal pardon in 1415 not a trace of Glyndwr could be found. Despite local traditions, his final resting place remains unknown.

The 'Pennal letter' was written in the name of Owain Glyndwr to Charles VI, King of France. In it Owain, styling himself Prince of Wales, promised allegiance to the Pope (in Avignon) in return for the French King's support of an independent Welsh Church, the foundation of two Welsh universities in Wales, and recognition of Owain's sovereignty. As far as is known, the French King never replied to the letter, or ever ratified any agreement with Owain. The document is dated at Pennal, near Machynlleth, on 31 March 1406, and probably represents the summit of Owain's power and influence.

The pardon of Sir William Stanley after the battle of Shrewsbury, 3 November 1403.

In the wake of the battle of Shrewsbury those who had fought for the Percys and survived the engagement naturally sought royal pardons. One of these was Sir William Stanley. The Stanleys had become one of the leading families in Cheshire and Lancashire during the course of the fourteenth century. This rise to prominence had been based very much on service within the Black Prince's administration and through the acquisition of extensive landholdings in the region.

After the Black Prince's death, the Earldom of Chester had passed to his grandson, Richard II. Richard had subsequently built up an extensive network of royal servants within the region. As tensions in the Kingdom grew during the 1390s, Richard had recruited widely within the Earldom. Considerable support for the deposed King persisted there even after 1399. Although Prince Henry had been created Earl of Chester by his father, Henry IV, it appears that not all of those who transferred into the service of the Prince were wholehearted supporters of the House of Lancaster. In fact, chroniclers reported the success with which Sir Henry Percy was able to recruit in the shire, a point reinforced by the very close correlation between the origins of many of the rebels and the actual route taken by Percy's force in July 1403.

Sir William Stanley's reasons for rebelling against Henry IV are at best uncertain. Stanley was a kinsman of Prince Henry's household steward and had much better access to the Prince's patronage than his contemporaries. The only immediately obvious reason appears to be the service ties forged with Sir Henry Percy. Stanley had been retained by Percy, serving him in the Welsh Marches. In 1402 he had then been sent to relieve Beaumaris by sea. In the event, it seems his involvement with the rebels was not held against him because he was granted a royal pardon in 1404.

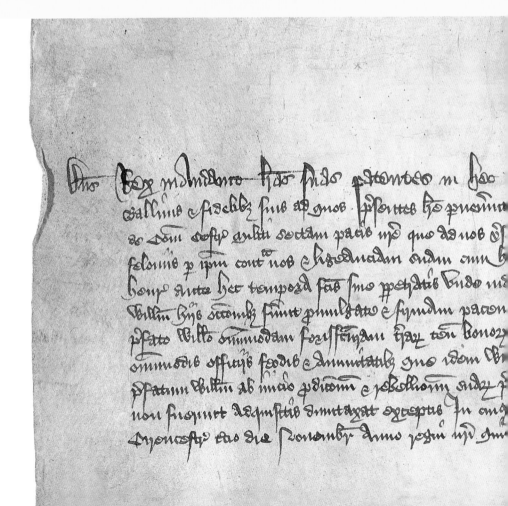

THE PARDON READS:

The King commands by his letters patent [document from a sovereign conferring a right] in these words. Henry, by the grace of God, King of England and France and Lord of Ireland to all his bailiffs and faithful subjects to whom these present letters come. Greetings. Know that we by our special grace have pardoned William de Stanley of the County of Chester, knight, prosecuted for breaking our peace, of all treasons, insurrections, rebellions and felonies committed and perpetrated by the same against us; and so we have pardoned his allegiance to Henry Percy the son, now deceased, and other of our rebels of the faction of the same Henry before this time, whereof the same William was adjudged, accused, or appealed, and also for any outlawries [being excluded from the protection of the law] which might have been proclaimed against him for these reasons, we grant him our lasting peace and have pardoned, granted and remitted to the aforesaid William all his forfeited, goods and chattels which should pertain to us from the abovesaid causes, excepting all offices, fees and annuities which the same William has for the term of his life, and also all goods and chattels acquired by the present William from the commencement of his aforesaid treason and rebellion to this point which goods and chattels of his before his said rebellion excepting those which were not purchased or demised [granted to others].

5 'Vadia Guerre' ('The Wages of War')

A list of Prince Henry's household men who served him during the Welsh rebellion, c. 1402–1405.

The practical – as opposed to the symbolic – importance of the household of the Prince of Wales was more than demonstrated by the rebellion of Owain Glyndwr. The Prince had already drawn men from the Duchy of Lancaster and the Earldom of Chester into his personal service. His household formed the basis of his military forces employed against the Welsh rebels and many who fought for him in Wales later fought for him as King in the French wars.

The Prince was surrounded from an early age by men of considerable military experience. One of these was the tough figure of Sir John Stanley, the final entry on this particular folio. He was the son of a minor Cheshire landowner. Having made a favourable marriage he emerged as a leading landowner in Cheshire and Lancashire. However, Stanley's fortunes were founded largely on his military and administrative skills.

His ability was first recognized when Richard II appointed him Lieutenant of Ireland in August 1389. The change of dynasty improved rather than hampered Stanley's rise in the world. He obtained some of the lands of the Earl of Salisbury who had rebelled against the King in 1400. Stanley served two further terms in Ireland and was, according to Irish chroniclers, particularly avaricious.

Stanley became Steward of the Prince's household in 1403. It was in this capacity that he served the Prince in Wales as well as at the battle of Shrewsbury in 1403. In that encounter Stanley was seriously wounded in the throat. As a reward for his service he was granted the lands of his nephew, Sir William Stanley, who had rebelled with the Percys against the King. Stanley's prominence continued to grow. In 1405 he became Steward of the King's household. His favour reached its peak in 1406 when he was granted the Lordship of Man. He died in 1414.

THE ENTRY RELATING TO SIR JOHN STANLEY READS:

John Stanley knight, steward, for his wages at 4s; 14 esquires and 50 archers at the accustomed wages, namely from the aforesaid 18 April until 15th day of May for 28 days until the day of account; by indenture dated the last day of June in the aforesaid year. £58 16s

This leather pouch was used to store Exchequer documents, including the one featured here. The pouch would normally have the contents listed on the front for ease of reference.

Idem computat soluisse Dns Thome comiti Wygorn pro ba[n]... suis ad vj s viij d ... j militis ad ij s xxxviij scutifer[is] quolib[et] ad xv d ... sagittar[iis] quol[ibet] ad vj d per diem ... a xviij die Aprilis Anno xx henrici quarti post conquestum quarto usque ad xv diem maij proximo Sequente vtroq[ue] die computat[is] per xxviij dies siue Indentur[am] ————

Idem p constlib[us] badijs suis j militis xxxviij scutifer[is] et ... sagittaro[nd] per me ... xij die Junij anno predicto et ... de July proximo Sequente per ... dies vtroque die computat siue Indentur[am]

Johanni ... Assheton pro badijs ... scutifer[is] ... sagittar[iis] ... badia consuet vt supra videl[icet] a p[re]d[ic]to viij de Junij ... x diem July et xxviij dies vtroq[ue] die computat per Indentur[am] dar[e] xij die Junij anno quarto

Willmo dno de Talbot p badijs ij scutifer[is] et x sagittar[iis] ad badia consuet videl[icet] a predicto ... die Aprilis usq[ue] ...dem xv diem maij p xxviij dies vtroq[ue] die computat per Indentur[am] dar[e] xxvj die Junij anno p[re]dicto

Idem p bad[ijs] ... ad ij s xij scutifer[is] et ... sagittar[iis] ad bad[ia] consuet de supra videl[icet] a predicto xiij die Junij usq[ue] ...le diem eiusdem mensis p xviij dies vtroq[ue] die computat per eadem Indentur[am]

Eidem pro badijs suis xv scutifer[is] et ... sagittar[is] ad badia consuet vt supra videl[icet] a ij die July usq[ue] xviij diem eiusdem mensis p xviij dies vtroque die computat per eadem Indentur[am]

Johanni Tucher Dns Daudeley p badijs suis ad iij s xx scutifer[is] et ... sagittar[is] ad badia consuet videl[icet] a predicto xiij die Junij usque xxvj diem eiusdem mensis p xviij dies vtroq[ue] die computat per Indentur[am] dar[e] xij die Junij a[nn]o predicto

Ricardo dno de Gravnstde pro badijs ij scutifer[is] et xl sagittar[iis] ad vadia consuet videl[icet] a xxij die Junij usq[ue] vltimum diem eiusdem mens[is] p x dies vtroq[ue] die computat per Indentur[am] dar[e] xx die Junij anno predicto ————

Johanni Stanley militi Seneschallo p vadijs suis ad iij s xvj scutifer[is] et ... sagittar[iis] ad vadia consuet videl[icet] a p[re]dicto xviij die Aprilis usq[ue] xv diem maij p xxviij dies vtroq[ue] die computat per Indenturam dar[e] vltimo die Junij anno predicto ————

...vj s viij d ...

Dns patrie ...

Harlech Castle in North Wales was one of the strongholds built by Edward I in the late thirteenth century to keep the Welsh population in check, and had become a symbol of English dominance in the principality. It was captured by Glyndwr in 1404 and not recovered by the English until 1409. The fall of Harlech marked the end of the Welsh revolt.

THE PRINCE'S ROLE IN DOMESTIC POLITICS

After 1406, with Glyndwr's rebellion in Wales easily contained, the Prince emerged as a leading political figure in England. By December 1406 he had started to attend meetings of the King's Council in London. His influence steadily increased over the next few years. In 1409 the Chancellor, Thomas Arundel, Archbishop of Canterbury, resigned. Tension had been growing for some time between Chancellor and Prince. Power now shifted in the Prince's favour. In 1409 he was appointed Warden of the Cinque Ports and in 1410 he became Captain of Calais. The King's declining health gave him a further advantage. With the support and assistance of his kinsmen, Henry Beaufort, Bishop of Winchester, John Beaufort, Earl of Somerset, and Thomas Beaufort, later Earl of Dorset and Duke of Exeter, the Prince was able to assume leadership of the Council and became the dominant force in domestic politics.

Between 1410 and 1412 the principal issue facing the Council was relations with France. Internal faction-fighting had made that realm extremely unstable. After the assassination in the streets of Paris of Louis, Duke of Orléans, in 1407, by supporters of John, Duke of Burgundy, the situation had deteriorated further. It was into this conflict that the English were now drawn. Apart from concerns this might have on English trade with the Low Countries, Henry IV and the Prince were both keen to settle outstanding

Archbishop Arundel shown preaching the cause of Henry IV. Arundel had been banished by Richard II for his part in the noble opposition to his rule, but was reinstated by Henry IV on his accession to the throne, and became a leading political figure during the early years of the Lancastrian dynasty. He died during the first year of Henry V's reign.

A knight with a sword, and a shield decorated with crows, c. 1405. The knight's helmet, known as a *bascinet*, has the visor raised. It is fitted with its own mail guard, known as an *aventail*. Over his torso, he also appears to be wearing a *jupon*, a type of close-fitting padded coat. This type of armour was typical of the late fourteenth and early fifteenth centuries. By the battle of Agincourt in 1415, however, knights and men-at-arms were primarily dressed in full plate armour, although they still wore *bascinets*.

English territorial claims in France. According to the terms of the Treaty of Brétigny of 1360, France should have conceded Aquitaine in full sovereignty on condition that kings of England abandoned their claim to the French Crown.

With these issues in mind negotiations were opened with both the Burgundians and the Armagnacs, the name subsequently given to the party led by the assassinated Duke of Orléans whose son had married a daughter of the Count of Armagnac. In 1411 the English entered into negotiations with the Armagnac representative, the Duke of Berry. French attempts to include their allies in the negotiations were unacceptable to the English, as was their wish to include Normandy as one of the parts of France to be included within any truce agreed. That would, after all, have closed a possible invasion route to France. From the Burgundians the English sought a marriage for the Prince and help against Orléans to recover the possessions they demanded by right.

Although the negotiations with the Burgundians ended with vague promises of mutual support, the Prince and the Beauforts were sufficiently tempted to send an expeditionary force under the Earl of Arundel to assist the Duke of Burgundy. The English subsequently distinguished themselves in the key engagement at St Cloud. However, by November 1411 the King was well enough to resume control of affairs. In an embarrassing reversal of policy, he sent his son, Thomas, Duke of Clarence to aid the Armagnacs in 1412. This second expedition was no more than a profitable raid into Anjou and the Orléanais, and eventually both the Armagnacs and Burgundians paid him to return to England.

Relations between the Prince and his father had become strained during the final years of the reign. Later chronicles mention the Prince's wild streak and his tendency to play practical jokes, although there is no real historical basis for these stories. More serious, however, were the hints about the Prince's disloyalty to the King. In one account the Prince is said to have tried on the crown whilst his father lay asleep in bed. However, his father woke up, caught him in the act, and rebuked him for his actions. Although the King and Prince were reconciled, it is likely that relations continued to be tense until the King's death in March 1413. However, the rebirth of the English spirit was about to happen.

The Road to Agincourt: England's Finest Moment

HENRY THE KING

By the time of his accession to the throne in 1413, Henry was a man who knew how to lead others and who expected to be obeyed. Aged 26, contemporary descriptions of him about this time suggest he was a man of above medium height, with a strong but not outwardly muscular body. Few failed to be impressed by his dignified conduct and bearing as King. Yet Henry was very much a soldier at heart and his reputation was primarily based upon that. The King was to spend over half his reign on campaign, and for much of that time he led the life of the plain soldier. At times his commitment to the pursuit of a just war against France was to verge on the obsessive. However, this single-minded determination strengthened his reputation in England. Henry's bravery was universally acknowledged. By his death, he had become one of the greatest warriors of the Middle Ages.

The battle of Agincourt, 25 October 1415. A nine-teenth-century copy of a medieval illustration. In the background, underneath the banner on the right-hand side, Henry V is shown leading the English army. The French army is shown in retreat. In the foreground English archers inflict heavy casualties on the French knights.

Eighteenth-century engraving of Henry V by George Vertue (1684–1756). Henry, represented in a less austere fashion than his medieval portrait, is shown wearing a crown, a richly jewelled chain, and carrying an orb.

THE LOLLARD PROBLEM

Almost immediately after his coronation, however, Henry was faced with a rising led by the Lollard sympathizer, Sir John Old-castle, Lord Cobham. The spread of Lollard beliefs had caused

33

Monumental brass of Agnes Jordan, the last abbess of Syon Abbey. The Bridgettines were a religious order of cloistered nuns founded by St Bridget of Sweden in 1344 and approved by Pope Urban V in 1370. The order lived according to the rule of St Augustine, supplemented by constitutions drawn up by Bridget, and was designed to embody the highest ideals of contemporary piety, untarnished by complacency or corruption.

Syon Abbey was initially founded on the Middlesex bank of the Thames, roughly opposite Henry's palace at Shene [Sheen]. The location proved unsuitable and within a few years it was moved to the site now occupied by Syon House. The foundation charter of Syon of 3 March 1415 provided that the monastery should have an abbess and 59 nuns, 25 religious men of whom 13 were to be priests, four deacons and eight laymen. The brothers and sisters lived in separate courts, but shared a common church. By the time of its suppression in 1539 the abbey had become the wealthiest nunnery in England, and also the tenth richest religious house.

increasing concern to the Church for it questioned the traditional authority of the Pope, the cult of saints, and the Virgin Mary. Itinerant preachers brought the message of the gospels directly to the population by delivering sermons in English. English translations were also printed and circulated. Moreover, Lollard views had found a sympathetic audience at Court. A distinct group of royal servants actively helped the Lollard preachers. Despite his education, Henry V was a conventionally pious man and attached great personal importance to established forms of worship. The sincerity of his views should not be doubted, nor the importance he attached to prayer and divine intercession in the affairs of men, which led him to make regular donations to the Church. Discover more about Henry's piety: document 6, *Henry's religious beliefs*.

Oldcastle was a veteran of the fight against Owain Glyndwr where he had earned the respect of Prince Henry. Nevertheless, his connections could not prevent his conviction for heresy in September 1413 before Archbishop Arundel. Sympathisers then allowed Oldcastle to escape from the Tower of London. From hiding in London Oldcastle organized a rising against the King. It failed miserably and many rebels were killed in a brief skirmish. Commissions of inquiry were organized across the country to investigate Lollard activity and to arrest principal suspects. In March 1414 a general pardon was issued to all participants in the rising if they gave themselves up. Oldcastle, however, remained at large until his capture and execution in December 1417. Read about attempts to apprehend Oldcastle: document 7, *The hunt for Sir John Oldcastle*.

Thomas Arundel, Archbishop of Canterbury, receiving and then presenting a book, *Scenes from the Life of Christ*. This representation is taken from William of Northampton's commentary on Clement of Lanthony's *Gospel Harmony*. Although Arundel is remembered chiefly for his defence of the Church against Lollardy, he was also a committed patron of learning and orthodox teaching of Christian doctrine.

Religious offerings made by Prince Henry to religious establishments in the Welsh Marches, c. 1402–1404.

Henry's attitudes towards religion were formed in his youth. He had received a wide-ranging education under the guidance of his father, Henry IV, and was therefore particularly well-informed about religious doctrine, liturgy and ceremony. Henry was reported by contemporary chroniclers to engage in private devotion and to patronize the most austere religious foundations.

In Henry's mind public worship and private devotion were intimately connected. He maintained an interest in religious affairs throughout his life and was especially concerned with monastic reform. This is best demonstrated by his ambitious building projects at the Carthusian house at Sheen in Surrey known as the Charterhouse and the Bridgettine foundation of nuns at Syon across the Thames. St Bridget of Sweden (1303–73) founded the order of St Saviour, known as the Bridgettines, for women who wished to live a contemplative life, as part of her vision for Church renewal.

A college of priests attached to each house provided sacraments and spiritual direction for the cloistered nuns and visiting lay people. The Bridgettines embodied the highest ideals of contemporary piety, untarnished by complacency or corruption. It was believed that the purity of their lives made their prayers more powerful, and therefore they attracted royal and aristocratic patrons like Henry V.

An important feature of late medieval religious practice was to make offerings to the Church. As the household accounts of Henry, Prince of Wales demonstrate, he was offering oblations (gifts) at the altar at the Monastery of Lichfield in Staffordshire and in the Church of the Preaching Friars

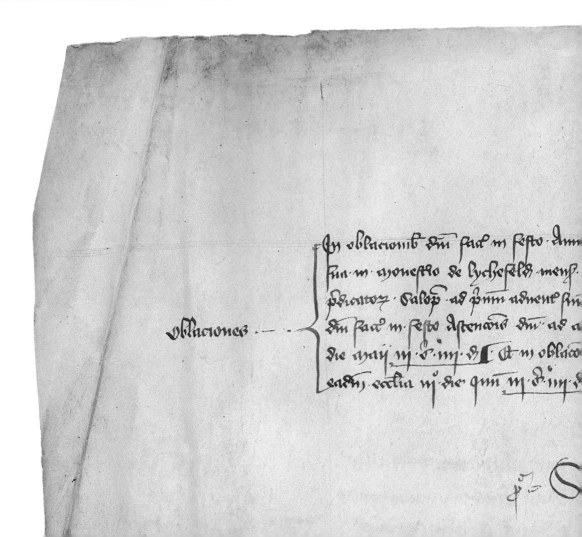

in Shropshire whilst directing military operations in Wales against Glyndwr.

The Welsh Marches were, in fact, an area where the heresy known as Lollardy had taken hold. A number of Henry's friends and associates who were thought to entertain Lollard sympathies were even from this region. As King, however, Henry allied himself firmly with the ecclesiastical authorities in the Kingdom and showed no tolerance towards the Lollards or their sympathizers – even those like Sir John Oldcastle, who had been his friend and associate in his youth.

THE DOCUMENT RELATING TO OBLATIONS READS:

And in oblations made by the Lord in his proper person at Mass during the Feast of the Blessed Mary, celebrated at the alter in the Monastery of Lichfield in the month of March – 3s. And in oblations made by the Lord in the Church of the Preaching Friars in the aforesaid Shropshire, upon his first arrival in Shropshire, in the aforesaid month of April – 6s 8d. And in oblations made by the Lord celebrated in his presence in the same church during the Feast of the Ascension of the Lord on 24th day of May – 3s 4d. And in oblations made at Mass at the alter during the Feast of Pentecost 3 June – 3s 4d.

Woodcut depicting the martyrdom of Sir John Oldcastle, taken from *Acts and Monuments* by John Foxe. Oldcastle, a former comrade-in-arms of Prince Henry in Wales, advocated Lollard views and was condemned as a heretic by Archbishop Arundel in 1413. He was finally taken to St Giles's Field in London where he was hanged from a new gallows, the 'Lollard gallows' as they became known, whilst a fire was lit beneath him.

Although Oldcastle's revolt presented little direct threat to Henry, it did focus the King's mind on issues of domestic law and order. In order to launch a successful campaign in France he needed to know that England could be left in a settled state. He therefore imposed a tough crack-down on crime and disorder. A substantial number of judicial commissions of inquiry were established to investigate offences. Their results were sent into the Court of King's Bench at Westminster for consideration. The small quantity of convictions, combined with the wide-ranging general pardon that the King issued, suggest that he was really attempting to restore observance of the King's peace through reconciliation as much as anything. Yet for some it was reconciliation at a price. The King needed men to serve with him in France. In some instances, the path back to royal favour would involve these men risking their lives on the battlefield.

THE FRENCH WARS BEGIN

Having satisfied himself that England was in a settled state, Henry could now turn his attention to France. English campaigns there during the four-teenth century had taken the form of raids known as *chevauchées*. These could last from a few weeks to a couple of months. Decisive battles were rare though and the French were never brought to the point of complete surrender. The new King adopted a different approach in a clear break with the past. Before contemplating send-ing over an army, Henry conducted a diplomatic offensive designed to gain support for a just settle-ment of English claims in France.

Medieval helmet known as a *bascinet, c.* 1430. The face would have been protected by a detachable visor with holes for sight and ventilation. These helmets were the first to be worn with complete suits of plate armour. Medieval armour from Western Europe was even exported to the Middle East and North Africa. This example was actually discovered in Kordofan in Sudan and probably came from France.

The King favoured strengthening ties with the Burgundians rather than the Armagnacs. Despite his preferences, Henry still kept his options open by treating for a truce with France and for marriage to the French Princess, Katharine. In 1414 Henry attempted to forge alliances with John, Duke of Brittany, Sigismund, Emperor-Elect of the Holy Roman Empire, and Ferdinand, King of Aragon. These attempts proved unsuccessful and by 1415 Henry had run out of patience. Embassies were sent to France twice within a period of less than eight months, but negotiations had achieved absolutely nothing: no territorial concessions or possibility of a marriage. The King decided that war was indeed the only way to achieve his ambitions.

It was in the preparations for his first major campaign that Henry displayed another of his talents, expert organization. Long and meticulous plans were made before his army departed across the

7 *The hunt for Sir John Oldcastle*

A proclamation by the Crown to the general public appealing for their help in apprehending the Lollard heretic, Sir John Oldcastle, c. 1416–17.

When Sir John Oldcastle was almost captured at Silverstone in Northamptonshire in 1414 by the authorities, he departed in such a hurry that he left behind him some of his arms and armour. Oldcastle was a tough, military veteran of the early fifteenth century. He had benefited from the Welsh revolt of Owain Glyndwr. He fought under the command of Henry, Prince of Wales and consequently formed a strong bond of friendship with him. At its heart lay a common chivalric outlook. Oldcastle subsequently took part in jousts at Lille in France in 1410. The following year he served with the English contingent sent to assist the Burgundians at the battle of St Cloud.

This friendship remained firm when Henry became King in 1413. Even when condemned as a heretic before Archbishop Arundel, Henry V did his best to balance his friendship with Oldcastle with his belief that the established Church should be defended against heresy. The King allowed Oldcastle time to reconsider his views from his prison in the Tower of London. Instead, the latter was dramatically rescued by sympathizers and went on the run.

Hiding in London, Oldcastle plotted an uprising. The King caught wind of the conspiracy and was waiting for the rebels when they gathered outside the city on the evening of 9 January 1414. In the resulting skirmish some were killed whilst many others were captured. Having escaped the débâcle in London, Oldcastle went into hiding again. He managed to lead a charmed life, staying one step ahead of his pursuers in the Midlands despite losing his arms and armour. In a desperate move to capture him, the authorities offered a substantial reward of 1,000 gold marks and an annuity of £20 per annum to any individual who cornered him, whilst cities and towns were offered tax concessions. Oldcastle avoided capture until 1417 when he was cornered at Welshpool in Powys in Wales. He did not surrender easily and was wounded in the fight. He was then taken to London and again condemned as a traitor. He was taken to Tower Hill for immediate execution under armed guard. To the end he maintained a bitter hostility to the established Church.

THE PROCLAMATION READS:

Be it known to all manner men on our sovereign lord's behalf Henry, King of England and of France, of Ireland that for as much as Sir John Oldcastle sometime called Lord of Cobham refuse nor will not resume nor sue to have none of the joys before his time by our aforsaid liege lord [sovereign] granted to all his liege people that have offended, but continued forth in his evil and cursed purpose to destroy this noble kirk [Church] of England and the King and his true liege people [people bound to give allegiance to the sovereign], our aforsaid sovereign liege lord has granted and grants to what man that he be that takes or may take from this day forth the aforesaid Sir John Oldcastle and keeps and brings him to the King he shall have and be truly paid of 1,000 marks of gold, a £20 of sure living yearly during his life. And if any city, borough or other town may take the aforesaid Sir John and keep him or bring him to the King it shall pay neither fifteenth, tenth nor tax during the King's life though any be granted in this land from thence forward. And also that we charge and command straightly to all the lords, officers and all other our liege men that they be helping, supporting and strengthening to his taker or to his takers whatever that he be or they be.

Be it knowne to alle men on oure souerayne lieve lorde behalf, Henry Kyng of England and
of Fraunce lord of Irlande that for als mykyll as John Oldcastell sometyme callid lord of
Cobham refusid nore wolnought peccaue nore sue to haue none of the seide before his tyme be oure
forsaide lieve lorde grantid to all his lieve peeple that hath offendid, bot contunued forthe in
his entent and conseid purpos to destroye the noble kyrke of England and the kyng and his wolle
lieve peeple, oure forsaid souerayne lieve lorde hath grantid and grauntys to what man that he
be that takys or may take fro this day forth, the forsaid John Oldcastell and kepe and
bryngys hym to the kyngis he sall haue and be the sikkyr parcel of C li marc of gold a to as oure
kynelos yerly duryng his lyne. And if any two thre or othir terme may take the forsaid John
and kepe hym or bryng hym to the kyng, it sall be asthappid and made free that sall paid nothing
yumzysms disme nor taxe duryng the kyngis lyne though any be grantid in this land the those
forsaide. And also that the chayre his comaud expressly to al the lordys officers and al othir
also lieve men that there be helpyng and socoryng and strenghyng to his taky or his takys
that any the he be or thay ben.

English Channel. The army was raised in the usual manner, by contracts between the Crown and captains, known as indentures of retinue. Discover some
of the problems of the indentured retinue: document 8, *The payment of wages.*

Henry, however, was determined to be thoroughly prepared. He ordered investigations into all the arms and armaments stored in every castle in the land, especially cannon, large gunstones and gunpowder. He also summoned the leading men from coastal ports to discuss logistics and cross-Channel transportation. Although the army's departure was temporarily delayed by the discovery of a poorly planned assassination plot centred around Richard, Earl of Cambridge, Henry, Lord Scrope of Masham and Sir Thomas Grey of Heton, the assembled fleet of about 1,500 ships finally set sail from Southampton in mid-August 1415.

The plan adopted in 1415 was very similar to that of Edward III in 1346. In many respects Henry wished to emulate and even surpass his great-grandfather. He chose to attack in the Duchy of Normandy, an area that could be separated easily from the French Crown. The initial destination was Harfleur, the most important port in the region and a known haven for French pirates. It was a strategically important site, standing at the mouth of the river Seine. Its well-defended walls meant that it could not be ignored if a successful invasion of the Duchy was to be conducted. The siege lasted five weeks and clearly demonstrated Henry's determination to succeed. As with the sieges he had conducted in Wales, Henry took great care to provide his army with all the equipment it needed. In particular, the heavy cannon transported to Harfleur inflicted considerable damage, as well as terrorizing the civilian population inside the town walls. Read a soldier's petition for help: document 9, *Serving King and Country*.

On 22 September Harfleur surrendered and in a carefully stage-managed ceremony the keys to the city were handed over to Henry seated under a canopy dressed in his royal regalia. The symbolism was apparent to everybody. The rebels were returning to the

Henry V's campaigns in northern France were marked by a number of sieges. The first, at Harfleur in September 1415, demonstrated the King's determination to succeed. Lasting five weeks, Henry employed cannon to terrorize and demoralize the population. The principal siege, however, was that at Rouen, which lasted from August 1418 until January 1419. In the scene shown here, contemporary with Henry's invasion of France, the attackers (carrying a French banner) are depicted using bows and arrows against the defenders. The latter retaliate with bows and arrows as well as rocks.

A Chancery petition by Sir Robert Cromwell and John English for payment of outstanding wages due to Sir William Cromwell, *c.* 1431–40.

By the fifteenth century the traditional means of raising troops for military service in France was through the indentured retinue. The indenture set out the strength and composition of a contingent, the period and place of service, the rate of wages and any bonus, compensation for loss of horses and equipment, and division of the 'spoils of war'. Naturally, one of the principal matters of concern for the retainer was payment. However, securing payment was not always a straightforward matter. As an inducement to securing service, as well as a sign of good faith, it was not uncommon for leading retainers to be given some form of surety or guarantee that they would be paid.

In some instances, the problems encountered with obtaining wages owed could drag on for years. This might arise either from the Exchequer refusing to pay or sometimes dishonesty by a companion-in-arms. This was the case with Sir William Cromwell of Nottinghamshire who never received his wages. It was left to his son, Sir Robert Cromwell to try to secure the wages due to his father. According to Cromwell's petition submitted to Chancery, Sir William Cromwell and Sir John Colville had both served in France with Henry V's brother, the Duke of Clarence. They had probably been part of the force that contracted with Clarence for the Agincourt campaign in 1415. Clarence's retinue numbered 240 men-at-arms and 720 archers.

As surety for the payment of their wages, Cromwell and Colville had been given a gold jewel with precious stones inset. Cromwell was apparently owed £38 7s but he had died before receiving payment. Colville, in the meantime, delivered the jewel to the Exchequer and collected the sums owing to both himself and Cromwell, which he then kept.

Sir William Cromwell's wife, Margaret, had obviously died before she had managed successfully to collect what was due. Now it was down to their son, Sir Robert Cromwell. He was the cousin of Ralph, Lord Cromwell, the highly placed member of the household of Henry VI. His chances of securing a favourable outcome through the exertion of private influence were now much greater. Sir Robert's appeal was made sometime before 1440 when mainpernors [guarantors] for both Cromwell and English appeared in Chancery, suggesting that the issue of non-payment of wages had lasted for approximately 20 years.

THE PETITION READS:

Beseeching meekly Sir Robert Cromwell knight and John English, executors of the testament of Margaret Cromwell, executrix, of the testament of Sir William Cromwell knight, that where as the said William Cromwell knight and John Colville knight were waged [paid] to go beyond the sea in the time of King Henry the Fifth in the company of the Duke of Clarence that last died; and in surety of their both wages, there was delivered to the said John Colville a jewel of gold garnished with precious stones as it appears by the writing under the seal of the said John Colville more plainly, the wages of the said William Cromwell amounting to the sum of £38 and 7s; as it appears by the same writing the said John Colville delivered the said jewel to the Exchequer after the death of the said William Cromwell, the wages of £38 and 7s not paid nor never like to be paid with out your good and gracious help in this case. Wherefore please it to your goodness considering these premises and how your said suppliants now have no remedy against the said John Colville by the Common Law to grant a writ of *sub poena* directed to your said John Colville to appear before you at a certain day by you limited [appointed] in the Chancery under the pain of 100 marks, there to be examined of these premises and after that to proceed as faith and conscience asks in these parts in the reverence of God and way of charity.

9 Serving King and Country

A petition appealing for alms by an old veteran of the French wars, Walter Orpington, c. 1449–53.

Whereas the majority of nobles, knights, esquires and gentlemen who fought in France could probably manage financially in their old age, the ordinary soldier found it much harder to provide for himself once his military career was over. Many had served in France throughout their adult lives. Some had suffered very debilitating injuries as a consequence of their service. A petition, for example, from a soldier called Thomas Hostelle who fought in Henry V's campaigns, related how he had been blinded in the eye by a crossbow bolt at the siege of Harfleur and then had his hand smashed at the battle of Agincourt. The chances of obtaining any employment thereafter would have been slim indeed.

Walter Orpington's petition, made sometime between 1450 and 1453, stated that he had faithfully served both Henry V and Henry VI for over 36 years. Based on his own evidence he probably served right up to the moment Normandy was lost to the French in 1450. Like Hostelle, Orpington had been at Harfleur, as well as many other places in Normandy and Lancastrian France. Orpington was certainly a career soldier. He had clearly enjoyed a wide-ranging career and had experienced both the positive and negative effects of warfare abroad.

The few details about his service which he provides suggest that his experiences were not unusual. The common soldier typically served under a number of different commanders during the course of his life. The men who served at the siege of Harfleur and at Agincourt generally went on to garrison those towns which were captured by Henry in his later campaigns. Orpington was undoubtedly stationed in various garrisons and fought in different field armies. It must have been whilst on campaign that he was captured and put to ransom. This was his financial undoing. Any means of support that he might have had had been used to regain his freedom. His only means of supporting himself in his old age was by charitable donations.

THE PETITION READS:

Meekly beseeching unto your poor and continual orator, Walter Orpington, that how be it your said beseecher has continued and abided in the wars of our sovereign lord the King in the realm of France by the space of 36 years and more; and there continually during the said time has done good and true service to his power and might as God knows, that is to say, to the King's father that now is, in his life at the siege of Harfleur and in divers and many places of France and Normandy, and since unto our sovereign lord the King now, without going out of the said realm of France and Normandy; and in this time has often been taken prisoner and lost great goods so that he is now fallen in great age and poverty and has little therewith to help and sustain him. Please it therefore your gracious lordship the premises [matters] tenderly considered to grant unto your said poor beseecher such gracious letters patent [document from a sovereign conferring a right] by which he may ask and take the alms of the people of the realm of England, there as he shall suppose most profitable and expedient for him towards the helping and relieving of his poor state, for goodness, love and in way of charity.

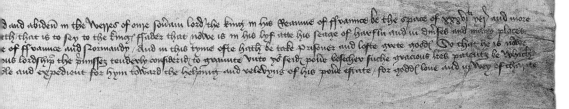

allegiance of their rightful lord. In keeping with his claim to be the rightful ruler of the Duchy of Normandy, Henry ordered that the inhabitants of Harfleur were to not to be molested in any way. Only those who had actively resisted him were expelled. Even these were escorted safely out of the town. This sent out a clear signal. The inhabitants of the Duchy would be treated justly; otherwise they would suffer forfeiture and confiscation of their property.

The capture of Harfleur was only the first stage in Henry's plans to reclaim his rightful inheritance in France. It is unlikely that he intended to do much more than establish a firm base in Normandy at this stage from which to launch future campaigns. The fact that within a couple of weeks of the fall of the town Henry was inviting English merchants to settle there suggests that he was planning further military activity in the region. He was planning to return and was taking measures to ensure that the local economy did not suffer in the meantime.

THE BATTLE OF AGINCOURT

Of more immediate concern was how to return to England. After summoning a war council the King decided to march to Calais rather than return directly from Harfleur. Similar marches by Edward III in 1346 and the Black Prince in 1356 had resulted in the French bringing the English to battle, at Crécy and Poitiers respectively. Such historic precedents were known to Henry before he set out. Once again he was making an attempt to emulate his illustrious forebear.

The march began at the end of the first week of October. Henry was leading an army of about 6,000 men and expected to reach

Edward III crosses the Somme during his French campaign of 1346. His army of about 4,000 men-at-arms and 10,000 archers had landed in Normandy in mid-July 1346. After ravaging the Duchy the King was intercepted by Philip VI of France with about 12,000 men-at-arms. Edward turned sharply northeast-ward, crossing the Seine at Poissy and the Somme downstream from Abbeville, to take up a defensive position at Crécy on 26 August 1346. The English won an impressive victory in which the power of the longbow over cavalry was visibly demonstrated. Over 1,500 French knights and esquires were killed.

Calais in eight days. Good progress was made. Although shadowed by a French
force the English encountered no significant opposition. However, they soon
learnt that the French were holding the crossing over the river Somme, including the crucial ford at Blanchetaque. Forced to march further to the south-
east, the English crossed the Somme at Bapaume. Sir Gilbert Umfraville and
Sir John Cornwall were sent to secure a bridgehead at the crossing. This in

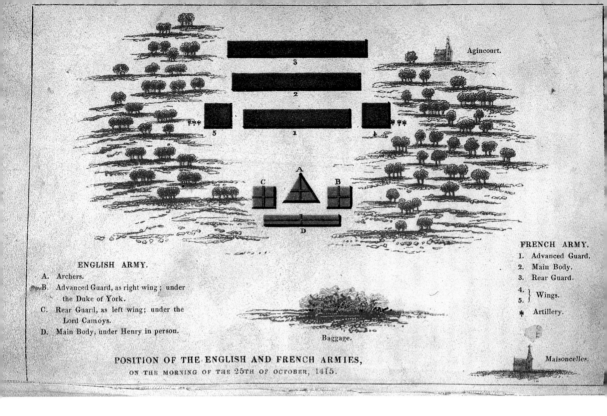

Agincourt.

ENGLISH ARMY.

A. Archers.
B. Advanced Guard, as right wing; under
    the Duke of York.
C. Rear Guard, as left wing; under the
    Lord Camoys.
D. Main Body, under Henry in person.

FRENCH ARMY.

1. Advanced Guard.
2. Main Body.
3. Rear Guard.
4. } Wings.
5. }
⚔ Artillery.

Baggage.

Maisoncelles.

POSITION OF THE ENGLISH AND FRENCH ARMIES,
ON THE MORNING OF THE 25TH OF OCTOBER, 1415.

An old representation of the battle of Agincourt. Although deployment of the three French divisions is probably correct (one behind the other with crossbowmen possibly identified here as Wings), the English army is incorrect. The main army is shown behind the vanguard (right) and rearguard (left) with the archers in between them. Historians now believe the main army replaced the archers' position here, and the archers were split equally on the wings and stationed behind sharpened stakes.

itself was a heroic feat. The causeway had first to be repaired and even then horsemen could only cross one at a time. All the while the English were conscious that the French could arrive at any moment.

Soon after their crossing, French heralds approached announcing that the Duke of Orléans, the Duke of Bourbon and Charles d'Albret, Constable of France wished to challenge the English to battle. The English chose not to take up the challenge and pressed on towards Calais, wearing part of their armour in case of sudden attack from the much larger French army which was now trailing them. On 24 October, shortly after crossing the Ternoise, the English had their first glimpse of the French. One chronicler called it as a swarm of locusts. The moment of truth had arrived.

On the orders of the King, the English army spent the evening in complete silence in the orchards and fields of a small village at

Maisoncelle. Henry had already released his French prisoners on the condition that if the English won the forthcoming battle, they would return to captivity. There was also a very practical reason for doing this: to prevent French prisoners attacking his army from the rear. The French, by contrast, could be heard close by making merry and acting like an army that had already won. Early in the morning of Friday 25 October the King, fully armed, heard three masses. After putting on his helmet, to which had been fixed a rich golden crown, he mounted a small grey horse and ordered the army to take position in the field of battle.

Henry had positioned his army for maximum defence. To the left and right were woods. In the woods to the left lay the village of Agincourt. In front was an open area, recently ploughed, which became narrower towards the end occupied by the English. As tradition dictated, the King occupied the centre, the Duke of York, in command of the vanguard, on his right, and Lord Camoys, in charge of the rearguard, on his left. Henry arranged his force of 900 to 1,000 unmounted men-at-arms in three traditional 'battles' (or divisions) across the entire width of open ground between the woods. His 5,000 archers were divided equally on the wings. Henry remained prominent at the front of his army, motivated not only by his own sense of chivalry but also by a desire to deliberately draw the French into the range of his archers. See who served with Lord Camoys at Agincourt: document 10, *A medieval retinue.*

The French army consisted mostly of unmounted men-at-arms dressed in heavy steel armour with very small numbers of archers and crossbowmen to

Memorial brass of Thomas, Lord Camoys and his second wife, Elizabeth, widow of Sir Henry Percy, known as 'Hotspur'. Camoys was a seasoned military campaigner. He commanded the rearguard of Henry's army at Agincourt and was positioned on the left on the battlefield. In recognition of his martial exploits he was elected a Knight of the Garter in 1416.

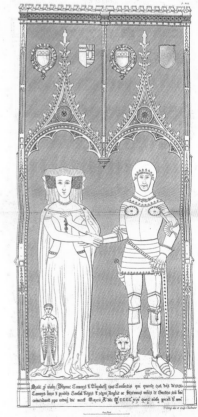

The military retinue of Thomas, Lord Camoys,
8 July 1415.

In the eleventh and twelfth centuries the feudal
system first introduced by the Normans into England
required tenants to perform unpaid military service for
their lord as one of the conditions for holding their land.
By the fourteenth century this form of service had largely
been replaced by money payments or rents instead. It
seems to have resulted from the military requirements of
Edward I in his Welsh and Scottish wars. The traditional
county levies were unwilling to serve outside their locality
even when promised payment. It therefore became
necessary to find alternative means of raising men.

The practice of drawing up an indenture [agreement]
between a captain and soldier was probably initiated
during the reign of Edward III when significant bodies
of men were required to pursue the King's territorial
ambitions in France. These indentures were standardized
documents dealing with all aspects of service. In the
fifteenth century troops for service abroad were raised
by this same system. A muster would be taken before
the retinue departed for France and again after its
return to England. The document shown here is the
copy that was submitted to the Exchequer for auditing
purposes. It was annotated to indicate those who fought
at Agincourt as well as those who had died at Harfleur.

The personal contingent brought by Thomas, Lord
Camoys to France is a typical reflection of the range
of men that were brought together by a captain. Men
served with a captain for a variety of different reasons.
Some were simply attracted by the pay; others were
attracted by the reputation and status of the captain;
whilst some were often connected personally to the
captain, perhaps in his household or on his estates.
Simon Brocas, who served as one of Camoys's men-at-
arms, might well have been one of the latter. He was
from a gentry family resident in Hampshire and would
probably have been known to the Camoys family who
were from the same region. Brocas, however, did not
survive the French campaign. An annotation against
his name on the retinue list states that he died in the
town of Harfleur. At the other end of the spectrum
were individuals like Geronet du Bayon, probably a
professional soldier from English-held Gascony.

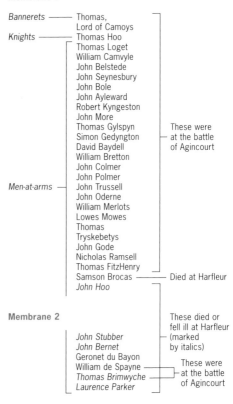

THE NAMES ON
THE MUSTER READ:

Membrane 1

Bannerets — Thomas, Lord of Camoys

Knights — Thomas Hoo

Men-at-arms —
Thomas Loget
William Camvyle
John Belstede
John Seynesbury
John Bole
John Ayleward
Robert Kyngeston
John More
Thomas Gylspyn
Simon Gedyngton
David Baydell
William Bretton
John Colmer
John Polmer
John Trussell
John Oderne
William Merlots
Lowes Mowes
Thomas Tryskebetys
John Gode
Nicholas Ramsell
Thomas FitzHenry
Samson Brocas — Died at Harfleur
John Hoo

These were at the battle of Agincourt

Membrane 2

John Stubber
John Bernet
Geronet du Bayon
William de Spayne
Thomas Brimwyche
Laurence Parker

These died or fell ill at Harfleur (marked by italics)

These were at the battle of Agincourt

Archers
Henry Goldrynge
William Strode
John Prior
John Pygot
Richard Atkyn
Henry ate Ryge
John Norreys
Nicholas Spray
Roger Edward
Richard Cadwell
Thomas Hunt
Richard Burdon
John Crescy
Thomas Coke
Henry Smyth
John Tyler
Simon Holand
John May
Henry Crispe
William Oldham
Roger Boteler
Thomas Russell
John Mayland
John Turnour
John Ambrace
Thomas Howdon
William Carpenter

These were at the battle of Agincourt

More Archers
John Balderby
Robert Forte
Robert Dene
John Perpoynte
John Chapman
John Pycton
William Bernard
John Lytster
Robert Coke
Henry Charps
Robert Appelby
Richard Kyng
John Gander
William Galnum
John Padley
John Morer
William Turner
Thomas Sadler
John Hipstnum
John Codyngton
Nicholas Turner
Richard Wykham
John Hosyer
John Charette
John Durnwell
Lowes Lawrence
John Turndale

These were at the battle of Agincourt

Thomas Cemaum

William Bourgh
John Armorer
John Fote
John Petyrffeld
John Darnwell
Philip Hownet
Gregory More
John Mannynge
John Spycer
Stephen Abyrcourt
Robert Hardynge
William Waryn
John Merden
John Colyers

These five indicated by an asterisk were at the battle

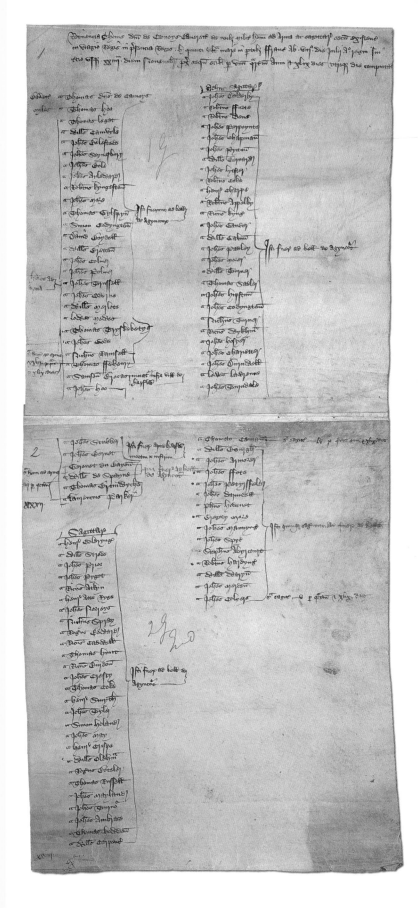

support them. The Constable, d'Albret, and the Marshal, Boucicaut, had devised a plan of attack to defeat the English by employing their vanguard of dismounted men-at-arms supported by crossbowmen on the flanks and at the front. Yet the French commanders were divided amongst themselves and would not make the first move. D'Albret and Boucicaut were overruled by the Dukes of Orléans, Alençon and Bourbon who decided to launch an all-out attack on foot.

The three French 'battles' were deployed one behind the other and only the third included cavalry. The intention was to overwhelm the English. Realizing this, Henry broke the deadlock and ordered the English to advance. His army moved to within 200 yards of the enemy where his archers then drove their stakes into the ground to protect them from cavalry attacks and commenced to fire volley after volley of arrows at the massed French men-at-arms. This had an almost instantaneous effect. The French cavalry charged but the sodden ground and deadly volleys of arrows shattered their assault. They were soon driven back on to the bulk of the French army which had begun its own advance.

This general advance was an unmitigated disaster. The French men-at-arms, forced closer and closer together by the narrowing ground, were met by English forces holding full-length lances with archers in support behind them. When the two lines clashed the sheer weight of French numbers initially told. The fighting was at its most intense under the banners of the three 'battles'. During this hand-to-hand fighting Edward, Duke of York was killed. Henry himself came under ferocious attack and one blow even dented his helmet. Nevertheless, the English line held and they were able to gain the upperhand. English archers were also able to join the fray by attacking the French from the flanks with arrows, swords and axes.

A dramatic representation of Henry V at Agincourt by Sir John Gilbert. Chroniclers recorded how Henry remained a conspicuous figure at the head of his army, seeking to inspire his men against the French enemy facing them. Henry featured prominently in the fighting during the battle and was even struck on his helmet during a ferocious French attack.

The increasingly demoralized French started to flee, causing great confusion amongst their comrades who were advancing to join the *mêlée*. Although about two-thirds of the French army was destroyed, Henry still faced the third French 'battle' led by the Counts of Marle and Fauquembergue which had so far taken no part in the encounter. At the same time reports reached the King that the French were attacking the baggage train. Concerned that his army might be caught in a trap, and still heavily outnumbered on the battlefield, Henry ordered the execution of his French prisoners. Read about a disputed ransom: document 11, *Agincourt prisoners*. In the event, the third French 'battle' did not attack. Realizing that it was not going to attack, Henry called the heralds before him who, in their traditional roles, had been observing the battle. From them he obtained a recognition that victory was his. On being told that the nearest village was Agincourt, he decided that the battle should be named after it. The significance of the English victory at Agincourt was not lost on contemporary chroniclers, who recognized the superiority of English tactics, organization, and above all, the leadership of Henry V.

A complaint in Chancery by John Craven and Simond [i.e. Simon] Irby that they had been cheated of the ransoms due to them from their Agincourt captives, c. 1415–26.

One of the debates surrounding the battle of Agincourt is the order that Henry V apparently gave to execute enemy prisoners when he feared an attack from the rear by French forces. He was criticized by some commentators for violating the chivalric code which stated that unarmed prisoners should be treated according to the well-known conventions of warfare. However, it should be remembered that the French were fighting under their war-banner known as the 'oriflame', which meant that no quarter would be granted to English prisoners.

Contemporary English chroniclers reported that some men-at-arms refused to become involved in the slaughter of prisoners. It is unlikely that they were concerned about the proper rules of chivalry though. Whilst it would be wrong to view the principal motivation of men to serve in the wars of Henry V as profit, it was undoubtedly a factor in the minds of some. Consequently, the attitude of men-at-arms at Agincourt was much more likely to have been shaped by a concern to protect potential ransoms.

In fact, as this example demonstrates, prisoners were certainly taken at the battle and subsequently put to ransom. Arranging for a ransom was far from straightforward though. There were plenty of opportunities for some part of the

process to go wrong. Whilst raising a ransom could be financially crippling for those nobles or knights forced to mortgage or sell their lands, not all captors enjoyed the fruits of their military endeavours. Some, for example, found themselves defrauded. John Craven and Simon Irby alleged that William Bukton had done just that. He had seized their prisoners, put them to ransom and then freed them. Craven and Irby had not given up though. Learning that a portion of the ransom money had been placed in the hands of an officer of the Treasurer of Calais, they petitioned for that money to be given to them. Sadly it is not known whether they ever received the money they believed was theirs by right.

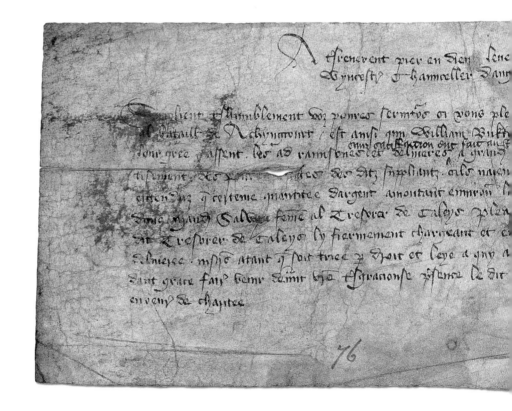

THE COMPLAINT READS:

Supplicating very humbly your poor servitors [servants], if you please, John Craven and Simond Irby that where as they captured certain prisoners at the battle of Agincourt, William Bukton, esquire, by force and to the injury of all the said prisoners of the said supplicant, and against your grace, put them to ransom and freed them (without satisfaction made thereof to the King or paid by them), to the great damage and prejudice or right of our very sovereign lord the King, and against the future prosperity of the said supplicants if they do not have your very helpful assistance and service in this present matter. And whereas the said supplicants have heard that a certain quantity of money amounting to about the sum of 200 marks, a portion of the ransom of the said prisoners, has been delivered into the hands of Salvayne, Farmer [Revenue Collector] to the Treasurer of Calais, please it Reverend Father to grant to your said supplicants writs directed to the said Treasurer of Calais faithfully charging and directing him to deliver the said sum kept in the hands of his said Farmer and not delivered, which belongs to the gentlemen by right and law, and which our said sovereign the King has himself desired and spoken of, of your very ability and grace, to require the said William Bukton to come into your presence and declare to you the names of the said prisoners, for God and in way of charity.

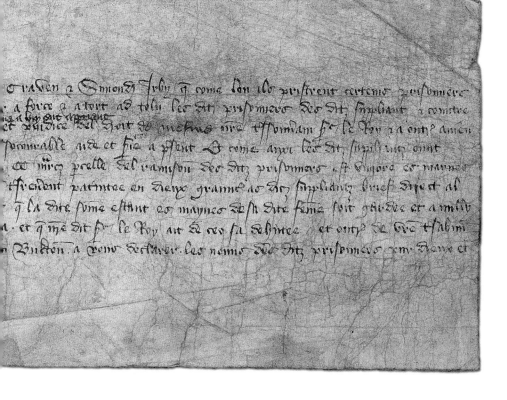

ent
ys
a
nt
to
tt
ne
is
au
ris.
tz
elles
cel

stat
stre
uet
qlz
uen
is
tre
our

Pour lan mil.cccc.et sept.
Coment le duc dorleans eut par
lottroy du roy son frere la duche dac
qutaine.Et lors furent faittes treues
entre le royaulme de france et dangle
terre. Chappitre.xxiiij.

A Dual Monarchy:
Henry, King of England
and Regent of France

THE CONQUEST OF NORMANDY

After his victory at Agincourt and safe return to England in November 1415, Henry remained in the Kingdom for the next two years, leaving the defence of Harfleur and the Channel to his uncle, Thomas Beaufort, Duke of Exeter and his brother, John, Duke of Bedford. During 1416 the French launched a number of offensives against Harfleur, determined to recover their national pride. In August a fierce naval engagement took place just off the town. English chroniclers, including John Hardyng who undoubtedly took part in the fighting, stressed the length of the battle and the amount of casualties on both sides.

Even during his stay in England, Henry's mind was concentrated on how to make his next move against the French. On 1 August 1417 he launched his second campaign across the Channel. An agreement made with John, Duke of Burgundy in October 1416 had paved the way for the King's new venture. In it the Duke recognized Henry's right to the throne of France, a right confirmed by his victories in battle. Moreover, it stated that once Henry had conquered a sizeable part of France, the Duke would formally recognize Henry and his heirs as his sovereign lord. He would then undertake to help him in secret ways. In reality this treaty gave Henry little practical assistance. Nevertheless, it did demonstrate that he was now determined to conquer France.

Peace made between England and France. The Treaty of Troyes was agreed by Henry V of England and Charles VI of France on 21 May 1420. By the terms of the treaty Henry V married the King of France's daughter, Katharine, and became Regent of France during his lifetime. On the death of Charles, the heirs of Henry and Katharine would become kings of England and France. Nevertheless, considerable opposition remained in France, gathering around the Dauphin Charles who had been disinherited.

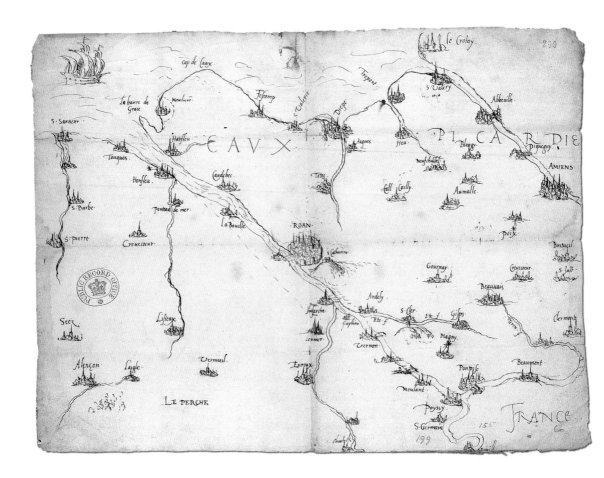

Unlike his attack on Harfleur and previous English campaigns, the 1417 invasion was intended from the very outset to be a long-term enterprise. The aim was to conquer territory systematically which meant a lengthy process of subduing key strategic sites before moving on to the next. As soon as he landed, Henry advanced west towards Caen. The town, second in importance after Rouen, was an important administrative centre that would serve as a base from which to launch further campaigns. The siege lasted about two weeks during which the walls were subjected to a severe barrage. The town was an important symbol for Henry. Within the precincts of the Monastery of St Etienne lay the remains of Henry's ancestor, William the Conqueror. The chronicler Walsingham recounts that a monk, hoping to save the tomb, came to the Duke of Clarence and warned him of plans to destroy it. Clarence acted swiftly. He led a personal attack on a section of the town's walls and the town fell before any major destruction could take place.

From Caen Henry decided to head south. The King's Burgundian alliance meant that his eastern flank was secure from attack. His south-western flank was also secure after he signed truces with Anjou, Brittany and Maine. During this period Henry was able to mop up resistance. The town of Falaise had been deliberately by-passed. The siege of Falaise began at the beginning of December but it took two-and-a-half months before the town finally ca-pitulated. The town offered stout resistance to the English, and suffered considerable damage during the course of the siege. Like Caen, Falaise also had symbolic importance to Henry for it was the birthplace of William the Conqueror. Yet its capture meant that he was now able to divide Normandy into two and gradually extend his control within the Duchy.

A sixteenth-century map of Normandy indicating the principal cities, towns and rivers within the Duchy. In the centre of the map is shown the city of Rouen, on the river Seine, the ancient capital of the Duchy, which fell to Henry V in 1419.

From this point on Henry initiated a dual process of conquest and estab-lishment of administrative control. During the spring of 1418 he began to organize the distribution of lands and estates confiscated from his 'rebels' to his English and Norman supporters. See how Normandy was ruled: document 12, *Resurrecting the Norman Rolls*. In the same period, between March and August 1418, the entire western half of Normandy came under Henry's authority. At the same time Henry advanced his forces into the eastern part of lower Normandy so that by mid-summer almost the whole of Normandy on the left bank of the Seine was in the King's hands.

At the beginning of August Henry ordered the siege of Rouen. This was one of the major events of the time, lasting until the middle of January 1419, and was reported as far afield as Venice. It was a prize that Henry was determined to win at all costs. Rouen was the capital of Normandy. He who possessed the city and its strategically important castle was traditionally entitled to call himself Duke of Normandy. It was the centre of administration and justice within the Duchy, with its own mint. Moreover, it was also the seat of the Archbishop of Rouen, whose ecclesiastical authority stretched across Normandy.

Typical examples of entries from the main series of governmental records of the Duchy of Normandy, 1418.

When Henry V secured control of Normandy he revived and modified an ancient series of official records which had previously ended with the loss of the Duchy of Normandy to the French King in 1204. Under Henry V, these Norman Rolls mirrored the Patent Rolls kept in Chancery at Westminster, but contained business exclusively relating to the Duchy.
The Norman Rolls included a variety of different matters, the most common being grants and confirmations of estates to those who had voluntarily surrendered to him or his commanders, grants of offices within the administration there, grants to his followers of the castles and estates of those Normans who were killed or remained in open rebellion, letters of safe-conduct and protection, commissions to array, and presentations to ecclesiastical benefices.

Reading from top to bottom in this particular extract for 1418–19, John de Bienfaite was granted the fee of Bouchart; Richard Hemingburgh was granted the fees of Conurignie and Neusy; John du Fay, esquire, and his heirs were restored to their lands in the Duchy; the Keepership of the Seal in the Viscounty of Evreux was granted to John de Court; Sir John Steward was granted the castle of Neuilly Levesque; Joan de Juvigny, formerly the wife of Sir William le Moigne, was granted all her rents, dowry and possessions in the Duchy; Richard de Benzeville, chaplain, and his heirs, were restored to their inheritance in the Duchy; two safe-conducts were granted, one to Peter Longlois and another to John de Londois; and finally, the temporalities of the Priory of d'Annebaut were restored.

Henry V was particularly keen to secure the allegiance of the native Normans and this extract contains several such confirmations. Where he could not, however, their lands were granted to reliable Englishmen. Richard Hemingburgh was one individual who benefited from Henry V's patronage. Hemingburgh was probably from the village of Hemingburgh in North Yorkshire and was typical of the gentlemen and esquires who joined in the King's enterprise across the Channel. He first appears serving under Henry Lord FitzHugh as a mounted man-at-arms at Falaise on 26 August 1418. He then went on to serve with Sir William Huddleston as a mounted man-at-arms at Alençon on 5 February 1421 and with Thomas, Earl of Salisbury as a mounted man-at-arms at Falaise in May 1423.

This grant to Hemingburgh was a valuable reward for his service to the Crown – as long as Normandy remained safe and secure.

THE ENTRY RELATING TO RICHARD HEMINGBURGH READS:

The King to all whom these present letters come, etc, greetings. Know that of our special grace and for good service that our beloved liege, Richard Hemingburgh, esquire, has done and will do to us in the future, we have given and granted to him the fee and land of Conurignie that lately belonged to John de Melle, to the value of 150 francs per annum; and also the fee of Neusy that lately belonged to the Lord of Battiebant, to the value of 100 francs per annum. To have and to hold by the aforesaid Richard and the heirs male of his body, up to the value stated abovesaid, of us and our heirs by homage and rent, to us and our same heirs, at our castle of Cadomo [Caen] of one poleaxe at the Feast of the Nativity of the Lord each year, and also by performing other services due and customary forever, etc. Providing always that the same Richard and his heirs aforesaid, or their deputies in their absence, might be summoned there and then to the castle or town of Falaise with men, etc; and notwithstanding that fee and lands aforesaid or any parcels of the same given and granted to any other person by us before this time; notwithstanding our intention that the aforesaid Richard, etc, having by colour of the presents any other houses, lands or other possessions in our town of Falaise, etc, or in our town of Codomo. Witnessed by the King at the Castle of Codomo 24th day of May.

p Joh'e de Bienfaite — R. Omnibus ad quos &c salutem. Sciatis quod nos de gratia nostra speciali et pro bono et acceptabili servicio quod dilectus et fidelis noster Johannes de Bienfaite miles nobis
impendit et impendet in futurum dedimus et concessimus ei feodum de Boncachart quod valoris trescentarum librarum turon' per annum dum ante existit
81 ut dicitur. Habendum et tenendum feodum predictum prefato Johanni et heredibus masculis de corpore suo exeuntibus de nobis et heredibus nostris per homagium ac
reddendo ——— nobis et eisdem heredibus
nostris apud castrum nostrum de Cadomo unam lanceam ad festum sancti Michaelis singulis annis necnon faciendo alia servicia inde debita et
consueta imperpetuum. Reservatis &c. Proviso semper quod feodum predictum vel aliqua percella eiusdem alicui alii persone per nos ante hec tempora
date et concess' non existat. In cuius &c. T. R. apud Civitatem de Lisieux xxx die Maii. p ipm Regem.

p Ric' Hemyngbroghe — R. Omnibus ad quos &c salutem. Sciatis quod de gratia nostra speciali et pro bono servicio quod dilectus ligeus noster Ricardus Hemyngbrugh armiger nobis
impendit et impendet in futurum dedimus et concessimus ei feodum et terram de Compigne quae nuper fuerunt Johannis de Mello ad valorem
8 centum et quinquaginta francorum per annum necnon feodum de Nonfy quod nuper dominus de Sacriebant [?] tenuit ad valorem centum
francorum per annum. Habendum et tenendum prefato Ricardo et heredibus suis masculis de corpore suo exeuntibus usque ad valorem supradictum
de nobis et heredibus nostris per homagium ac reddendo nobis et eisdem heredibus nostris ad castrum nostrum de Cadomo unum polaxe ad festum Natalis
domini singulis annis necnon faciendo alia servicia inde debita et consueta imperpetuum. Reservatis &c. Proviso semper quod idem Ricardus et heredes
sui predicti aut eorum deputati ibidem in adsencia sua castro seu ville nostre Falesie cum gentibus &c. quociens ibi fuerint premuniti et quod dictum
feodum et terra predicta seu aliqua parcella earundem alicui alii persone per nos ante hec tempora data et concessa non existant. Intencionis
tamen nostre non existit quod prefatus Ricardus &c aliquas domos terras aut alias possessiones infra villam nostram Falesie &c aut infra
villam nostram de Cadomo colore presencium habeat quovismodo. In cuius &c. T. R. apud castrum R. de Cadomo xxviij die Maii. p ipm R.

p Joh'e du Ffay — R. Omnibus ad quos &c salutem. Sciatis quod nos de gratia nostra speciali et ad supplicacionem Johannis du Ffay armigeri ac Petri fratris eius mater ligeorum nostrorum
dedimus et concessimus eis omnes hereditates ac alias possessiones suas quascumque infra ducatum nostrum Normannie quas ipsi tempore ultimi
descensus nostri in ducatum nostrum predictum habuerunt et tenuerunt. Habendum et tenendum eisdem Johanni et Petro hereditates et possessiones suas predictas
eodem modo quo ipsi tempore descensus nostri predicti habuerunt et tenuerunt de nobis et heredibus nostris per homagium ac faciendo alia servicia
inde debita et consueta imperpetuum. Reservatis &c. Proviso semper quod hereditates et alie possessiones predicte seu aliqua parcella earundem alicui
alii persone &c. nec quod iidem Johannes et Petrus aliquas domos terras aut alias possessiones infra villam nostram Falesie quas ad opus
nostrum fortificare intendimus aut infra villam nostram de Cadomo colore presencium habeant quovismodo. In cuius &c. T. R. apud villam
de Bernay —— die Junii. p ipm Regem.

p Joh'e le Compt — R. Omnibus ad quos &c salutem. Sciatis quod de gratia nostra speciali concessimus dilecto nobis Johanni le Compt officium custodis sigilli ad obligaciones
in vicecomitatu de Evereux. Habendum quamdiu nobis placuerit cum vadiis feodis et proficuis eidem officio antiquitus consuetis. In cuius
&c. T. R. apud villam de Nonburgh [?] octavo die Junii. p ipm Regem.

p Joh'e Tyrwhyt [?] — R. Omnibus ad quos &c salutem. Sciatis quod de gratia nostra speciali concessimus dilecto et fideli nostro Johanni Tyrwhyt capitaneo castri nostri de
Tilly [?] levesq' [?] quod ipse quamdiu nobis placuerit colligat et recipiat singulis annis per manus suas vel deputati sui pro quo respondere voluerit
omnia proficua et comoditates provenientia de omnibus terris feodis ten' possessionibus maneriis redditibus et aliis pertinentiis dicto dominio
Baronie predicti castri pertinentibus ad solvendum vadia nostra consueta quinque hominum ad arma et quindecim architenentibus in castro predicto
pro salva custodia ac munitione et defensione eiusdem castri continue residentibus. Ita quod de surplusagio comoditatum et proficuorum predictorum
si quod fuerit nobis ad camaram compotorum nostrorum Normannie annuatim respondeat ut est iustum. In cuius &c. T. R. apud castrum
R. de Cadomo xxij die Maii. p ipm Regem.

p Johanna Inmgny [?] — R. Omnibus ad quos &c salutem. Sciatis quod nos de gratia nostra speciali et ad supplicacionem Johanne de Inmgny [?] que fuit uxor Guilli lemoigne [?]
chivaler' mater ligee nostre concessimus eidem Johanne omnes hereditates redditus dotes et possessiones suas infra ducatum nostrum
Normannie quas ipsa ante ultimum adventum nostrum in ducatum nostrum predictum tenuit et possidebat. Habendum pro termino vite sue pro servicia
inde debita et consueta de dono nostro. Dummodo tamen hereditates redditus et possessiones huiusmodi seu aliqua parcella earundem
alicui alii persone per nos ante hec tempora dati et concessi non existant. In cuius &c. T. R. apud castrum R. de Cadomo xj die
Maii. p ipm Regem.

p Ric' Benzeville — R. Omnibus ad quos &c salutem. Sciatis quod nos de gratia nostra speciali et ad supplicacionem Ric' de Benzeville capellani canonici de Bayeux
matri ligei nostri concessimus ei omnes hereditates suas quas ipse ante ultimum adventum nostrum in ducatum nostrum Normannie tenuit et
possidebat. Habendum et tenendum sibi pro servicia inde debita et consueta de dono nostro. Dummodo tamen hereditates predicte seu aliqua parcella
earundem alicui alii persone per nos ante hec tempora date et concesse non existant. In cuius &c. T. R. apud castrum R. de Cadomo
xj die Maii. p ipm Regem.

De salvo conductu Lenglois — R. per has suas patentes usque festum sancti Johannis Baptiste proxime futurum duraturas suscepit in salvum &c Petrum Lenglois usque presenciam
Regis veniendo et ibidem per eum cum diversis suis in comitiva sua remanendo. Proviso semper quod ipsi quicquid quod in Regis contemptum vel
preiudicium aut populi sui dampnum aliqualiter cedere valeat non attemptent nec fiat quomodolibet attemptari et quod ipsi nullum
castrorum seu villarum Regis firmatarum absque speciali licencia capitaneorum eorundem intrent quovismodo. In cuius &c. T. R. apud
castrum R. de Cadomo xj die Maii.

De salvo conductu Landois — R. per has suas patentes per idem tempus duraturas suscepit in salvum &c. Johannem le Landois usque presenciam Regis veniendo cum diversis
suis in comitiva sua ac equis rebus bonis et hernesiis suis remanendo. Proviso semper &c ut supra usque et quod ipsi nullum castrorum
&c ut supra. In cuius &c. T. R. apud castrum R. de Cadomo x die Maii.

De restitucione temporalium Innelsbourgh [?] — R. Omnibus ad quos &c salutem. Sciatis quod de gratia nostra speciali et ob divinum amorem ac alia pietatis opera que in prioratu Innelsbourgh [?]
de Mortaing fieri debeant plus solito augmentanda et ibidem laudabiliter manutenenda et sustinenda concessimus dilectis
nobis in Christo priori et conventui prioratus predicti omnia temporalia eiusdem prioratus infra ducatum nostrum Normannie
ad ipsum spectantia sive pertinentia. Habendum in sustentacionem divini cultus et aliorum pietatis operum predictorum de dono nostro

how erle richard was atte sege of Roan there set furst betwen the kyng
tent and seynt kateryns / And whan seynt kateryns was wonne he
was sette to kepe port charterhyse

THE SIEGE OF ROUEN

The siege of Rouen, as depicted in the *Beauchamp Pageant*, took place from August 1418 to January 1419. Henry V conducted the reduction of the city with typical ruthlessness. The city was placed in a stranglehold and slowly starved into submission. The fall of Rouen, the traditional administrative centre of Normandy, signalled the completion of the conquest of the Duchy. Here Richard Beauchamp, Earl of Warwick, is shown kneeling before Henry V. Thought to have been commissioned by Anne Beauchamp in honour of her father Richard Beauchamp, the fifth Earl of Warwick, the *Beauchamp Pageant* is a collection of late fifteenth-century manuscripts. The 53 line drawings, with small amounts of additional text, celebrate the life and deeds of Richard, and extol the virtues and ideals of chivalry and service.

The English established a cordon around the city. A ditch and bank were built around the walls, to protect their own army as well as keeping the city's population inside. Stakes were placed in the ditch to prevent horses being used. Henry also used the city's position on the banks of the Seine to his own tactical advantage. Whilst preventing the French from shipping in supplies and provisions by river, he brought in as much equipment as necessary from Harfleur. Henry was a master of psychological warfare too. Once during the siege he organized a 'phoney' battle between some of his men wearing the traditional red cross of England and others bearing the white cross of France. The citizens were so convinced they were saved that they started ringing the cathedral bells, only to have their hopes dashed once it was realized no relief force was on its way. Recognizing that they were not going to receive assistance from the Dauphin or any others, a group of citizens entered into negotiations with Henry in December 1418. After a lengthy series of talks the city finally surrendered on 19 January 1419.

On the diplomatic front Henry had been busy playing off the Armagnacs, more appropriately referred to now as Dauphinists, against the Burgundians. In May 1418 the Dauphinists had fled from Paris which came under the control of the Burgundians. Within a couple of months, however, they had both reconciled their differences. In July 1419, fearful of continuing English successes, the Burgundians had made an alliance with the Dauphinists at Pouilly-le-Fort. The aim of the treaty was simple. They both agreed to work together to expel the English. During the course of 1419 the English had extended their control up the Loire Valley to within a few miles of Paris itself. Henry was more than aware that control of the capital would solve many of his problems.

THE ANGLO–BURGUNDIAN ALLIANCE
AND THE TREATY OF TROYES

Once again, the torrid political state of France helped Henry achieve his ambition of securing control of Paris. At a meeting in September at Montereau, between Duke John of Burgundy and the Dauphin, the Duke was assassinated by the Dauphin's servants. This had clearly been a premeditated action on the part of the Dauphin, who showed no remorse whatsoever when he wrote to the new Duke a few days later. In fact he remained critical of the Burgundians, in particular their tendency to support the English.

Very soon after the murder, the English and Burgundians entered into complex diplomatic negotiations about the future of the French monarchy. After considerable internal debate amongst the Burgundians it was recognized that supporting the English was their most advantageous course of action. On 2 December Duke Philip of Burgundy issued letters from Arras acknowledging that Henry was to marry Katharine, daughter of Charles VI, and that their children would succeed to the French throne upon the death of the French King. On Christmas Day 1419 Henry issued letters patent agreeing to the concessions made by Duke Philip and agreeing, in turn, to support the Duke's rights in France. These articles were subsequently enshrined within the terms of the Treaty of Troyes on 21 May 1420. Henry was acknowledged as Regent of France during the lifetime of Charles VI and the Dauphin was cut out of the succession. The treaty went into great detail as to how Henry would rule for his father-in-law. In addition, all Frenchmen were to take an oath of acceptance of this treaty's terms. This done, Henry and Katharine were solemnly

Katharine of Valois, daughter of King Charles VI. The Valois dynasty ruled France from 1328 to 1589. Katharine was born on 27 October 1401 in Paris. Relatively little is known about her life. In 1420 Katharine was given in marriage to Henry V according to the terms of the Treaty of Troyes. The only issue of this marriage was the future Henry VI of England.

R: DE: FRANCE

b: LE: CINQVIESME:

Le premier chapitre de
mon stre comment se
roy se en ala a Rains sou
faire couronnier quel
que enps droit il seul
o nom
du pere
du filz
du saict
esperit de la glorieuse vi

cite marie de mon seigneur
sainct denis patron de fra
ce et de toute sa beatitude ce
seste. cy commencent les
cronicques et gestes du teps
de trescriftien roy de fran
ce Charles vij de ce nom fai
tes et compilees par moy
frere Iehan chartier religie
et chantre de segli se mons

The marriage between Henry V and Katharine of Valois, aged just 19, was conducted in the church of St John in Troyes on 2 June 1420. It was described as a low-key ceremony. After the sudden death of Henry V on campaign in France in 1422, Katharine was effectively exiled from court and denied access to her son. At some stage she formed a secret liaison with Owen Tudor, a Welsh squire serving in the royal house-hold. Their son, Edmund Tudor, Earl of Richmond was the father of the first Tudor king, Henry VII. Katharine died during child-birth in London in 1437.

betrothed by the Archbishop of Sens. On 2 June Henry and Katharine were married in a carefully stage-managed ceremony with very few guests, a recognition perhaps that this was, above all, a political marriage. Read Henry V's announcement of his marriage: document 13, *Katharine of Valois*.

The treaty and marriage received a mixed response in the Kingdom. Although welcomed in Paris it was received at best with caution elsewhere. The Dauphin and his supporters refused to accept it, of course. Many regions and towns in France declined to recognize its validity. Unperturbed, Henry allowed little time to elapse before he resumed military operations to conquer the rest of France and secure acceptance by force. See document 14, *The draft Oath of Allegiance in France*.

The announcement of Henry V of his forthcoming marriage to the French Princess, Katharine of Valois, 22 May 1420.

Although there was an ancient rivalry between the kings of England and France, the two royal houses had continued to intermarry throughout the Middle Ages. The marriage between Edward II of England and Isabella of France, daughter of Philip IV, however, had provided their heir, Edward III, with a claim to the throne of France after Charles IV had died without a male heir in 1328. Although the throne passed to his cousin, Philip of Valois, who became Philip VI of France, their rivalry subsequently sparked the beginning of the Hundred Years War.

On one level therefore, the marriage of Henry V to Katharine of Valois, daughter of Charles VI, was not out of the ordinary. However, the circumstances of the marriage and the resulting implications were far from normal. Edward III had sought to bring a halt to French interference in the affairs of Gascony for which kings of England were required to pay homage as vassals of the French kings. The solution he had come up with involved using his dynastic claim as a way of securing concessions. The Treaty of Brétigny, which was agreed with Philip VI in 1360, was designed primarily to bring about the end of a feudal dispute.

On the other hand, Henry V was seeking to settle outstanding English claims

that had actually been agreed in the Treaty of Brétigny. Moreover, the Treaty of Troyes turned the Treaty of Brétigny on its head by creating a dynastic settlement in favour of the English that also settled their outstanding claims in France at the same time. Furthermore, Henry V's intervention in French affairs came at a time when that Kingdom was being torn apart by internal faction-fighting and English assistance was being sought by the opposing factions. The marriage to Katharine, and Henry's obligation to enforce the settlement of the Crown on the heirs of their union, was essentially a dramatic solution for creating lasting peace between France and England.

THE ANNOUNCEMENT READS:

Right trusty and well beloved brother, right worshipful and worshipful fathers in God, and trusty and welbeloved. For as much as we knew well that your desire was to hear joyful tidings of our good speed touching the conclusion of peace between the two realms, etc. We signify unto you that worshipped be our Lord that of our labour has sent us a good conclusion upon Monday the 20th day of this present month of May we arrived in this town of Troyes and on the morrow we had a convention between our mother the Queen of France and our brother the Duke of Burgundy as commissioners of our part and the accord [treaty] of the said perpetual peace was there sworn by both the said commissioners in the name of our foresaid father and similarly by us in our own name. And the letters thereupon sealed under the great seal of our said father to us to hold and under ours to him to hold, the copy of which letters we send you closed in these to that end: that you cause the said accord to be proclaimed in our city of London and through all our realm that all our people may have verray [true] knowledge thereof for their consolation as well as keep it after as long thereunto them. Also at the said convention marriage was betrothed between us and our wife, daughter of our foresaid father, the King of France. And furthermore, for as much as we must by virtue of the said accord use a new style during the life of our said

father we send you a schedule within these [letters] our style that we will use hereafter both in Latin and in English and in French, charging you that in all things that pass during the time afroresaid as well under our great seal as all our other seals wherever it be and in proclamations you ordain that our style be used after the content of the said schedule, and that the scripture of all our seals be amended thereafter in all haste and so charge by our writs all our offices that this may long [pertain] to as well in England as in Ireland and in Guyenne [Gascony] for so we will ordain that it shall be done even under our signet in the said town of Troyes the 22nd day of May abovesaid, and as touching the scripture of the seals we feel [us semeth] that this word Regent may be known well enough.

To our right trusty and well-beloved brother the duke of Gloucester, Warden in our realm of England and to all the remnant [remainder] of our Council there.

Henry, by the grace of God, King of England, heir and regent of the realm of France and Lord of Ireland; memorandum, having been enrolled by virtue of letters of the privy seal of the Lord King from the Chancery of England, and filed in the same Chancery of the Lord King in this year. [Henry's style was provided in three languages.]

Right trusty and welbeloued &c. Ryght worschipfull and worschipfull fadres in god and trusty and welbeloued for as muche as we sore wole pat yowe desyre were to here joyfull tydyngs of oure goode spede touching ye conclusion of pees bi twix ye two rewmes &c. We signiffie vnto yow pat worschippede be oure lorde pat of oure labour hauy sene to a goode conclusion vpon moneday ye xxi day of pis pñt moneth of may we arryued in pis town of Troyes And on ye morow we hadden a comunicacion bitwix oure moder ye quene of ffrance and oure brother ye duc of Burgoyn as comissares of ye kyng of ffrance oure fader for his partie and we in oure psonne for oure partie and yaccorde of ye said pees perpetuele was pis day bi boye ye saide comissares yn name of oure forsaide fader And semblably by vs in oure owne name And ye saide acorde for þi enseled vnder ye grete seel of oure saide fader to be kepte and vnder oures to hym kepte ye copie of whiche we sende yow closed yn pees to þat ende pat ye do ye saide accorde to be proclamed yn oure citee of london and yelesewhere oure rewme þat al oure pueple may haue verray knowlege þof for yare consolacion as wel we kepe hit afty as longe as yt you avaylme Also at ye saide comunicacion was mariage bitrouthed bitwix vs and oure wyf doghter of oure forsaid fader ye kyng of ffrance And for þi now for asmuche as we muste by vertue of ye saide accorde vse a newe stile durynge ye lyf of oure saide fader we sende yow ma certule wiþin pees oure stille pat we wol vse heraf boye in latine in englyssh and in ffrensch chargeyng yow pat al thyngs pat passey durynge the tyme aforesaide as wel vnder oure grete seel as al oure oþ seel what ealle her bee and inproclamacions ye ordeyne pat oure stille be kept aft ye contenne of ye saide certule And pat ye oþ scripture of alle oure seelis be amended aft yn al haste And so chargey by oure ire vs alle oure officé pat yis may long oure aft seel yn England as yn Irlande and yn Guyenne for oþ wol we ordeyne pat shalle doon heere yeuen vnder oure signed m we saide town of Troyes ye xxv day of may abouesaide And as touching ye scripture of ye seeles vs semeth yat ye . . . de Regent may be oute wel ynogh.

To oure ryght trusty and welbeloued brother ye duc of Gloucestr' wardein in oure rewme of Englande and to alle ye residue of oure consell yere.

Henricus dei gña Rex Angl' heres & Regens regni ffrance & Dñs hibñ.

Henry by ye grace of god kyng of England heyre and Regent of ye rewme of ffrance and lord of Irlande.

Henry par la grace de dieu Roy dengletre heyrer & Regent en Royaume' ffrance & seigneur dirlande.

Et memorand' qᵈ pmissa sunt ynrotulata virtute hñs depputato sigillo Dñi Regis Cancellar' Angl' Regin' & iij filiacis Cancellar' ipim Dñi Regis de hoc Anno psentis.

14 *The draft Oath of Allegiance in France*

A copy of the oath to be sworn by Frenchmen to Henry V, *c.* 1420.

The Treaty of Troyes and the marriage of Henry V and Katharine of Valois received a mixed response from the French populace. The treaty was ratified in the cathedral of St Peter in the name of Charles VI of France on 21 May 1420. By its terms, Henry V was acknowledged as Regent of that Kingdom during the lifetime of Charles VI and the Dauphin Charles removed from the succession.

One of the conditions of the Treaty was that all Frenchmen were to take an oath of allegiance to Henry V as Regent. A copy of this was subsequently preserved in Chancery in England. It laid out clearly what was expected of King Charles's subjects. Matters of State were entrusted to Henry. Consequently, Frenchmen were required to obey Henry and his heirs as if he was already King of France. They were to continue in their allegiance even if he fell ill or suffered any harm. They also had to agree not to provide any assistance whatsoever to the King's enemies – even if they were in the ascendancy. Finally, they were to do all in their power to resist any plots against Henry that were discovered by themselves or by others.

Although popular in the capital, Paris, the Treaty's reception elsewhere was more muted. In addition to the Dauphin and his supporters other areas and towns in France refused to accept it. Key individuals like the Count of St Pol, the Burgundian-appointed Captain of Paris, were replaced because of reservations they expressed about taking the oath of allegiance. Even Dijon, one of the Duke of Burgundy's principal towns, had to be visited specially by the Duke and persuaded to comply. Opposition was also voiced by churchmen like the Abbot of Beaubec, who claimed that the peace was false because the Dauphin had been robbed of his right to the throne by force. Designed as a means of ending the war, the practical outcome of the settlement was more than apparent to all: war would continue until one side was victorious.

THE DRAFT READS:

You swear and promise that the most high and very mighty Prince, Henry, King of England, is Governor and Regent of the realm of France, and of the public affairs of the same; and you are also ordered and commanded to serve and obey him humbly, loyally and diligently, in all matters touching and concerning the governance and monarchy of the realm of France, and of the public affairs subject to my very high and very mighty Prince and sovereign lord, Charles, King of France. Item, that forthwith after the death of my said sovereign lord, Charles, King of France, you will continue to serve as loyal men, liege and true subjects of the said very high and very mighty Henry, King of England and of his heirs forever, and to have and accept and obey the same as your sovereign lord and true King of France, without question, contradiction or difficulty. And that you never disobey us either as King or Regent of France unless our sovereign lord Charles, King of France has spoken to the very high and puissant [powerful] Prince, Henry, King of England and his heirs. Item, that you do not serve or aid, counsel or assist, anybody but the said very high and very puissant Prince, Henry, King of England – even if he loses life or limb, or is affected by bad health, or suffers harm or diminution [reduction] of his honourable person and estate, or because of other bad things you know about, or the distress caused by some other matter plotted against him, or plots you prevent insomuch as you are able to by sending messages or letters to him the sooner that you are able to do so. And generally you swear that without deceit or evil scheming you will look after and observe all the matters, points, and articles contained in the letters and appointment of the final peace made accordingly [i.e. Treaty of Troyes], between our sovereign lord, Charles, King of France and the very high and very puissant Prince, Henry, King of England; without ever deciding, directly or indirectly, publically or secretly, by some pretext heard or seen during that year, or that afterwards will come to pass or is agreed to, to protect the matters, points and articles abovesaid or contained within them, but in every possible way as long as you rightly can, to resist those actions which are clearly seen or attempted, or suffered to be made, or are attempted against these matters or points abovesaid or within them.

Vous Iurez et promettez que ...humble et tressouffisant prince henry Roy dangleterre ... a gouvernement ... Royne du
Royaume de france et de la chose publicque Iurerez et a ce mandement et commandement vous entendrez, obeirez
humblement loyaument et diligement en toutes choses touchans ... le gouvernement et Ryne dud Royaume
de france ... et de la chose publicque sereves a treshault et tresexcellent prince ... nre ... seign[eur] Charles Roy de france
... que ... apres le dect de mond[it] souverain seigneur Charles Roy de france ... vous ferez
loyaulx hommes liges et beaux subgitz dudit treshault et trespuissant henry Roy dangleterre et de ses hoirs perpetuelmet
et tiendrez come ... souverain seigneur a vray Roy de france ... sans opposicion ou difficulte aucune et vous...
... come vray Roy de france obeirez Et que Iamais a nul aultre come a Roy ou Royne de france nobeirez, Et non a
mond[it] souverain seigneur Charles Roy de france car aud[it] ... et puissant prince henry Roy dangleterre ...
vous ... que vous ne ferez ... conseil ou consentement que ledit treshault et puissant prince henry Roy
dangleterre perde la vie ou membre ou soit porté ou mannaisse ... en quel souffise dommage ou diminucion ...
pourroit estre honneur en chose quelconque, mais se vous savez ou cognoissez aucune telle chose estre voulu par...
ou machinee vous lempescherez en tant come vous pourrez et par vous mesmes par messagier ou lectre au plus
... le plus tost que ferez pourrez Et generalment vous Iurez que sans fraud ... ou malengin vous garderez
... ferez garder et obserer ce ... et apoinctement le ledit quy...
final soit vaurde et tenu entre mond[it] souverain seigneur Charles Roy de france et ledit ... et puissant prince henry
Roy dangleterre, Sans Iamais en ... ne aller Directement ou Indirectement publicquement ou secretement...
par quelconque couleur ou voye que ce soit ou puisse estre ...son ... consuire ... au amoindre des choses ...et
arrestez desuzd[it]s, ou Aucune Dicelle, mais en toutes manieres et voyes possibles tant de fait come de droit...
avons ... qui donront ou attempteront ou efforceront de faire venir ou attempter encontre le ... ou poinct...
dessusd[it]z, ou Aucune Dicelle.

10

The Dauphin and his supporters were in control of territory to the south and east of Paris, especially in the Seine Valley below Troyes. Accordingly, Henry set out on the campaign accompanied by Katharine and the Duke of Burgundy, taking the town of Sens before moving on to a much more difficult prospect, Montereau. This siege lasted several weeks, but once taken, Henry continued on to attack other Dauphinist garrisons to the south-east of Paris. The systematic reduction of enemy-held towns continued. On 1 December 1420 Henry and the two royal families entered Paris where they received a joyful welcome. On 1 December Charles VI, Henry, and the Dukes of Burgundy, Clarence and Bedford made a processional entry. On the following day Queen Isabeau, Queen Katharine and the Duchess of Clarence made their ceremonial entry together.

Henry had been in France since August 1417. He now decided that it was time to return to England. Moving back through Normandy he took the opportunity to settle affairs at Rouen. He met the estates of Normandy and the 'Conquest' lands, those lands which lay outside the Duchy. Taxes were raised and matters of government discussed. Henry also received the homage of Englishmen for lands and honours that were granted to them. Thomas Beauchamp, Earl of Salisbury, for example, gave his homage for the county of Perche. Content that affairs had been left in good order Henry and Katharine left for Calais. Learn more about Henry V's style of kingship: document 15, *The King's private memoranda*.

The royal party sailed from Calais, reaching Dover on 1 February 1421. From there they travelled to London. Leaving Katharine at Eltham, Henry supervised the preparations for the Queen's coronation. She was met by the Mayor and Corporation of London, as well as the Guilds, as she entered the city on 21 February. From

Scene depicting the storming of a castle. The attackers are shown using the method known as escalade – to attack the walls using scaling ladders or siege towers. This diversion allows an engineer to make a breach in the base of the wall. Surviving documents show that Henry V was very concerned to provide his army with all the equipment necessary to conduct an effective siege, from scaling ladders to cannon.

there she was shown to her lodgings in the Tower. On 22 February she was taken to Westminster to prepare. Katharine was crowned Queen in a carefully stage-managed ceremony at Westminster Abbey on 23 February. Henry, however, took no part in the ceremony and there is no record that he attended either her coronation or the sumptuous banquet that followed. Instead she was given pride of place at a feast attended by the King of Scots.

Henry spent the early months of 1421 putting the affairs of England in order. Inevitably he had lost touch with events at home. To this end he conducted a tour of the country from 26 February and only returned to London at the end of April. During the course of this progress Henry was brought news at Beverley in Yorkshire that his brother and heir, Thomas, Duke of Clarence, had been

killed in a battle at Baugé in Anjou by a combined Franco–Scottish army. After learning from French prisoners of an army close by, Clarence had rashly decided to force battle, unaware of the size of their army. Initially meeting only token resistance, the English had soon come up against the main body of a much larger opposition army. According to the chronicler John Hardyng, Clarence had explained to his commanders that he felt obliged to attack because he had not as yet won honour in battle, a veiled reference perhaps to his elder brother's achievements.

15 *The King's private memoranda*

A list of 'things to remember' dictated by Henry V to his secretaries, *c.* 1420.

Medieval monarchs, unlike those of today, were very much involved in the practical, day-to-day government of their realms. Henry V is one of the best examples of a ruler who was actively engaged in all aspects of administration and politics. He was constantly thinking about what needed to be done, even when he was on campaign. Like most individuals, though, he needed to keep reminders and had lists drawn up for that purpose.

The example here of his memoranda is a perfect illustration of a monarch in action. It was composed in late 1420, just before the King's return to England with his new bride. It is apparent from the language used, especially the use of 'mon' and 'ma' on several occasions within the document, that the King was dictating these points to a secretary. The latter then wrote down brief summaries of what he heard in French. Interestingly, the final two entries on the reverse of the folio are in English, in what appears to be a different hand. These were presumably written by another secretary when Henry thought of a couple of extra matters requiring his attention.

The document certainly demonstrates Henry's thought processes in operation. The fact that the fifth entry is struck through probably indicates that this point had already been addressed or was in the process of being seen to. The range of matters highlighted on the document covered every conceivable aspect of government: the third addressed the security of the Duchy of Normandy, the sixth dealt with payment of arrears of soldiers' wages, the eighth covered payment of wages and allowances to his Norman officials, the tenth made practical arrangements for government during his absence, whilst the eleventh finalized the instructions for diplomatic missions to other European states. Henry V was very much a 'hands-on' monarch.

THESE POINTS READ:

3. Item, touching my coming to England, to make the country secure, failing advice that Flanders [controlled by the Duke of Burgundy] is unable to swear, and therefore make an exception [guarantee] for the security of all things that have not been made secure, until everything is done.

6. Item, to order a man who will pay the surplus of wages that are owing in France, to have assignment [to be provided with funds] to pay 7 francs for 4 francs, or a noble for 4 francs, where the wages of France of 20 francs have not been paid; and these wages are for 600 men-at-arms, etc, and the garrisons of Montereau at 50 men-at-arms, and of the two towns against the 'Gastinois', and the castle of Meleun at 40 men-at-arms, etc.

8. Item, for advising on the payment of wages of the Chancellor, men of the council and all other officers, and some of them to have pensions.

10. And especially to give the form [of words] and instruction to the Chancellor regarding the way he is to announce there, and generally to bailiffs and all officers, that no one is to not understand or acknowledge those gifts made by me by my will and by the grace of God in this part.

11. Item, to give the instructions and letters that Sobertier is to have which he will swear in Lorraine.

35 43

Item dordonner quelle commission besongnera dapresent avec a lemisson de parovis

Item dordonner quelle Instruction et commission lambaxade de havane avec

Item pour envoier a Cambray pour les signes sur les hamberisons
et de luy mander quelles signes il font

It ys to speke to court for thabbot of Westm
It thider for the Rent of the chartour &c

2 Apl 1619   Memoires

Premierement demores a vente thaal en langue et par tout la on les fremens de la
paix, ne font point faict pour les prendre

Et p especial a Abbeville, monstreuill, devant mon retour vers Engleterre

Item pour toucher a ma venue en Engleterre le fait des fremens de la paix
et faut auffi q flandres na point Jure, et pour ce q pourveon en fremens
de tant venue q nont fait le fremens Justines q lz lont fait

Item pour les comment a Kalaiz et es marchez vont deffz

Item de faire ordonner po la venue de maistre Jehan de courres medecin en Engleterre
et pour son paiement de trestous

Item de ordonne en boure q passea le surplusfage des gaiges q sont donnes
en france d'escavoir pour maro 66 fl po iiij fl ou noble pour iiij fl la
ou les gaiges de france ne sont q 66 fl po parc et ce pour 66 homes darmes
et pour les garnisons de monstreuil i homes darmes, et de ces deux villes
teve gastmors et le chastel de mullein po homes darmes 30

Item dordonner q Kerma les deniers de reulx de france q p panvay a beau
faire z enole de thavere z horestor 36 po ames france

Item danssee sur le fait de gaiges des thanvelle gens du conseil et tout ault
offices et se aucune amont pensions

Item po estre en advertz sur le fait de iiij que seront mises en lieu de plennont 36

Et p especial de donne favour et Justiniceon au thanvelle au plenn favour en y a
et gnralement aux baillie z tout offices q nulle ne praigne congnoissance des
donne q p moy sont faict p le que q dru ma bonne suite en ce pars

It dordonne les Justiniceon z les q amea tolerance qui sont en lorvaine

It restablement po linstruction z aucuns reulx qui sont en espargne

a Ne[...]o

THE CONQUEST RESUMED

The psychological impact on the English of this defeat was considerable. It was only because of the skill and experience of the Earl of Salisbury that a complete rout was avoided. Fortunately the French were too disorganized to press home their victory and move on towards Paris. Henry refused to be panicked by events and continued on his tour. Although preparations were set in motion to raise money, men and equipment, he only began serious preparations for another campaign after returning to London. The response in some regions was lukewarm. In Lincolnshire Henry even ordered commissioners to inform him of those who refused to help. On 10 June 1421 Henry returned to Calais. Accompanying him were his brother, Humphrey, Duke of Gloucester, the Earls of March and Warwick, and James, King of Scots. Henry's loyal brother, John, Duke of Bedford remained in England supervising affairs there in anticipation of the birth of Henry's first child.

Henry had intended to deal with Dauphinist opposition in Artois and Picardy. Discovering, however, that they had laid siege to Chartres, he hurried south hoping that his presence would encourage them to lift it. He also visited Paris early in July to bolster confidence in the capital. Henry initially moved to attack the town of Dreux which was forced to surrender after a month's siege. During the course of the siege it was subjected to a ferocious bombardment, a sign of Henry's renewed determination to become the master of the situation once more. Henry's return had given the English fresh heart and drive. He met little opposition and eventually brought his army as far south as Orléans. By then, however, it had become apparent that his lines of communication were stretched to breaking point. His men were exhausted and were suffering from a lack of provisions and equipment. Recognizing his

The genealogy of Henry VI is presented in the shape of a fleur-de-lys supported by the King's uncle, Humphrey, Duke of Gloucester and his cousin, Richard, Duke of York. On the right-hand side is a banner bearing the arms of the King's wife, Margaret of Anjou, supported by an antelope.

own weak position and the French unwillingness to face him in battle, he returned north to Paris to consolidate English control in and around the capital.

The military situation threatened to deteriorate. The French had settled on a policy of avoiding battle, which meant that the English could not inflict one final defeat on them and achieve military and political supremacy. Moreover, the further south Henry moved, the closer he came to the heartland of Dauphinist territory. To be able to undertake a concerted attack he needed to be absolutely sure of his support. Already the Duke of Brittany had abandoned the English and Burgundians. Soon after his return to Paris, Henry decided to lay siege to the Dauphinist-controlled town of Meaux which was only 30 miles to the east of Paris. Henry clearly saw that eliminating this trouble-spot would

bring one aspect of the conflict with the Dauphinists to an end. The siege lasted from October 1421 until May 1422 during which period Henry also initiated an intense diplomatic offensive designed to secure assistance from the Emperor Sigismund and other German allies. Henry felt let down by those who had made encouraging noises but offered little practical assistance in his fight to win recognition of his rights in France.

During the siege, the King's only child was born. He was christened Henry in honour of his father. All the bells of

London were rung that day. In France the King and the English army besieging Meaux received the news joyfully. Shortly after the siege was concluded in May, however, the first signs of illness probably started to affect Henry. The 35-year-old King had lived the life of the soldier for many years, experiencing with his men the less-than-sanitary conditions. Now, it seems, the King succumbed to the same poor conditions. In June the seriousness of the situation started to become apparent. After agreeing to help the Duke of Burgundy relieve the town of Cosne, Henry quickly became too ill to ride and was taken on a litter to Corbeil, south of Paris. The King's weak state and high fever were such that physicians did not like to administer medicine to be taken internally. By this stage he was probably suffering from dysentery; at the very least a chronic intestinal condition.

THE KING'S DEATH

Whatever the truth, his condition deteriorated steadily as his strength and energy slowly faded away. True to his nature and temperament, Henry continued to play an active role in government. See document 16, *Swearing loyalty to Henry V*. Curiously, however, it was not until he recognized that his death was imminent that the King attempted to put his affairs into proper order. Henry is known to have made two wills. The first, in July 1415, as he prepared for his initial campaign in Normandy; the second, in June 1421, before going on campaign for the final time. Both were made before the birth of Henry's son and heir though. The King left detailed arrangements to the executors of his will for the administration of his lands, the considerable debts that he had built up, and for the construction of his tomb in Westminster Abbey.

It is only in the codicils he added to his will in August 1422 that Henry attempted to make arrangements for the government in England but these still remained vague and unclear. His brother, Gloucester, was to be placed in overall charge of England and the infant Prince. Exeter was to be governor of the

Prince's person and appoint his personal servants. Sir Walter Hungerford and Henry, Lord FitzHugh were to assist Exeter run his household. No arrangements, however, were made for the government of the French dominions or for the future conduct of the war. It was only after testimony was given to the minority Council in England that it became clear that Henry intended his brother, Bedford, to exercise authority in France until Henry VI came of age. The King died on 31 August 1422. When Charles VI of France died on 22 October 1422, the infant Henry VI became the first and last monarch of the two realms. The question remained, though, whether he would be able to defend his dual monarchy.

The west end of Henry V's Chantry Chapel at Westminster Abbey. On the right-hand side of the north turret (on the far left of this photo) is a cardinal, possibly Cardinal Beaufort, who oversaw the building project. The Chantry was designed to stand over the tomb at a higher level, spanning the ambulatory with a bridge, and was reached by two spiral staircases rising from the east end of Edward the Confessor's Chapel. Alongside this photo one can see the funeral armour of the King, namely his helmet, shield and saddle.

Ratification of the oaths of loyalty sworn to Henry V by two Gascon enemies, 16 January 1421.

Gascony (otherwise known as Aquitaine or by its English corruption, 'Guyenne') had belonged to the kings of England since the marriage of Henry II to Eleanor, Duchess of Aquitaine in 1152. Although the Duchy had relatively little direct relevance to the security of England, it had an immense psychological significance to the Crown and was of particular importance to English commercial interests through the wine trade. It had even been considered as a possible place from which to lauch a full-scale invasion of France in 1415. That, of course, had not happened. However, the Treaty of Troyes of 1420 had included no specific provision for the future absorption of Gascony into the French realm of an English-born king; the presumption being that it would remain a French province governed by representatives of English kings.

The Duchy was in a weak state at the end of Henry V's reign. Revenues had declined and its military defences were recognized to be in a poor state of repair. Set against this was the threat to security posed by the Franco–Castilian alliance and the possibility of a naval assault on the coast. Action against Valois France could only be realistically contemplated through diplomatic means until such times as the finance required for military conquests could be obtained.

Two months after the Treaty of Troyes was signed, John Tiptoft, Seneschal of Gascony was commissioned to receive all rebels who wished to return to English obedience. This was a clear indication of the English policy of conciliation. This policy, along with English successes in Normandy, encouraged the powerful Albret family to seek an accommodation with Henry V. In January 1421 an agreement was reached between Charles, Lord of Albret and his cousin Francis, Lord of

St Bazeille. The two lords agreed to perform liege homage to him as Duke. All privileges were to be restored to them. An order was to be sent to Tiptoft (see enlarged section), as Seneschal, that, once letters from the two lords confirming the agreement had been received, he was to restore specified lordships to them before Easter 1422, or earlier, if feasible. In return ducal lands held by them or their subjects were to be handed over. A payment of £1,000 by Albret, as guarantee for the observance of the Treaty of Troyes, was to be respited until the King visited Gascony and made his intentions clear. The agreement contained no reference to Henry's title as 'Heir and Regent' of France, simply to Henry as Duke. In the event, neither took the oath in person, nor were the proposed restorations effected. Despite this apparent setback, diplomacy still remained a tool used by Henry V and the minority Council which governed on behalf of his son, Henry VI.

A KEY CLAUSE OF THE AGREEMENT READS:

Item, that the Lord King restores the aforesaid Charles and Francis, the Lords aforesaid, of all lands, rents, possessions, down to the very smallest existing lordship (excluding other things previously granted) which an examination shows they are owed by law, and which are kept by subordinates; or which as with others (except the sum of £1,000 aforesaid) were granted in letters by the order of his Seneschal of Aquitaine; and upon these singular and present letters performed, concluded and ratified by the same deputies and procurators to receive letters for the same lordships of Le Breto and St Basilia; and also with others of this kind above to perform attested oaths of homage and

fidelity sealed under their seals, and all lands, rents, possessions, and lordships aforesaid to be restored and handed over in actual fact to the Lords.

The lord King will treat with lord, Sir John Tiptoft, his seneschal of Aquitaine, and will compensate the same for the lands, rents and lordships written below, which belonged to lords de le Breto and de Sancta Basilia, and are presently in the hands of the said seneschal, and by the feast of Easter 1422, or sooner if possible, he will cause the same lands, etc, to be restored to the said lords.

The Decline and Fall
of Lancastrian France

ENGLISH SUCCESS, 1422–29

Contemporary depiction of Joan of Arc with a copy of her signature alongside. After convincing the Dauphin Charles of her divine mission to drive the English from France, Joan was equipped with arms and armour, and a special banner for her to carry into battle. On one side of the banner were the words 'Jesus Maria' and a figure of God, seated on clouds and holding a glove. The other side had a figure of the Virgin and a shield, with two angels supporting the arms of France. Joan's inspired leadership forced the English to withdraw from the siege of Orléans. However, she was captured by the Burgundians in May 1430 and handed over to the English. In May 1431 she was burned to death at the stake in Rouen.

In the immediate aftermath of Henry V's death, new arrangements for the government of England during his son's minority were quickly made. Despite Gloucester's claims to be Regent, the Council and Parliament disagreed. He was instead confirmed as Protector and Defender of England and his authority was curtailed by a minority Council upon which sat another of the King's uncles, Cardinal Beaufort. The continuing rivalry between Gloucester and the Cardinal was to remain a feature of English domestic politics during Henry VI's minority and the early years of his majority.

In France, though, English fortunes remained in the ascendancy. Henry V's brother John, Duke of Bedford exercised the authority of Regent on the young King's behalf. Bedford regarded this as a sacred duty imposed upon him by his brother. In line with his brother's wishes, he immediately resumed the task of completing the conquest of Normandy and the other territories held by supporters of the Dauphin Charles. See document 17, *The Duke of Bedford's goods*.

Successful expeditions into Picardy were conducted in 1424. The resounding English victory at the battle of Verneuil in August of that year on the Normandy–Maine border reinforced this sense of supremacy. English plans became more expansive as they swept up the Seine Valley towards Paris and strengthened the western border

17 *The Duke of Bedford's goods*

An indenture for the safe delivery of a richly jewelled and decorated cross to Richard Buckland, Treasurer of Calais, 15 August 1433.

John, Duke of Bedford was the third son of Henry IV and ruled Lancastrian France from 1422 to 1435. All the sons of Henry IV were remarkable for their keen interest in literature and the arts. Bedford was a noted bibliophile and was able to read Latin and Greek classics in French translation. He even purchased the great library of Charles VI, which he housed in his mansion of 'Joyous Repose' at Rouen in Normandy. Bedford also commissioned illuminated manuscripts of his own. In addition to his literary interests, Bedford was noted for his piety. He founded two monasteries in Rouen, one belonging to

the French order of the Celestines.

Bedford's service in France saw him amass considerable personal wealth, but also numerous debts. A glimpse of this contradictory situation can be seen in the following indenture made at Calais in 1433 between Richard Buckland, Treasurer of Calais and one of Bedford's councillors, and Gilles de Ferieres, Keeper of Bedford's Privy Coffers. Ferieres delivered into Buckland's hands a magnificent cross of gold and silver garnished with a large quantity of sapphires, rubies and pearls. The upper section with the Crucifixion had a cross-legged Christ, fastened to the cross with three pointed diamonds, representing the nails. There were four angels, one at each terminal, and the Virgin and St John on

each side. At the foot of the cross was a reliquary with a joint of St George, whose cult was widespread in France as well as England. Bedford's cross represented Christ in a rock-crystal tomb, with the three sleeping soldiers and an angel seated on the tomb.

It is not known how this cross came into Bedford's possession, but it could have been part of the payment of the ransom for the Duke of Alençon following his capture at the battle of Verneuil in 1424. The cross was probably later used as security for Bedford's debts, including those amassed as Captain of Calais. It remained in the possession of Buckland and his heirs and was valued at 510 marks in 1456–57.

THE INDENTURE READS:

This indenture made at the Castle of Balinghem at Calais, 15 August, 1433, between the honourable man, Richard Buckland, esquire, Treasurer of Calais and Councillor of the very high and mighty Prince, the Duke of Bedford, Regent of the realm of France, on the one part, and Giles de Feriers, clerk and Keeper of the Privy Coffers of the same Lord on the other part. Witness that the said Buckland to have and receive in the said place and on the said day, of my said Lord the Duke, by the hand of the said Giles, one very beautiful and rich cross of gold and silver, belonging to the said Duke, which he had crafted in two pieces, whereof one of the pieces made the cross, and the other a foot, upon which he stood the said cross, the said cross garnished with 26 beautiful large sapphires, 17 beautiful large pink rubies, 50 beautiful large pearls and 3 pointed diamonds marking the nails of the cross of

the Crucifix, and there is a angel on the 4 corners of the said cross and Our Lady and St John at two of them and at the base of the said cross, a reliquary where there is one of the joints of St George. And on the said base is an image of Our Lord entombed in crystal, garnished there-about with 6 sapphires, 4 pink rubies and 24 pearls, and there are three characters of men-at-arms before the said tomb, and on the same, an angel. And the top of the base, where the said cross sits, is in the manner of a mountain enamelled in green. And the same cross is in two covers of leather. Which cross my said Lord the Duke delivered to the said Buckland for him to protect. In witness of which, this part of the indenture to remain with the said Giles, the said Buckland to send his signet seal [and] sign manual in the year and day abovesaid, signed Richard Buckland.

anc ... le comble entre ... Ricaro ... lenier ... est le ... ... anno ...
armes de mondit ... au ... conpte en sont pri[s] ... ... je ... ...
plett double darnes blanc por ... ... deus ... ... darnes
blanc vendus ... deus andres darnes ... en ... ...
En tesmoing de ce a ceste parce dendenture demon ... deus joinles ... ...
villes ... andrey led Chotinzham a ... ... lan ... jo ... ...

Aultre copie

Ceste endenture fait au chastel de balpnyhu lez calais le ... jo danst
lan ... m ... entre honorable home Richart Bokeland esmer esperier
de calais ... conseill ... de ... hault ... puissat prince mon ... le dic de
bedford regent le Royaume de france dune part ... villes de ferrers
clerc ... garde de joueaus coffres dicelluy ... dant part ... esmoing ... led
bokeland a en ... recon en lad place ... led jo ... de mond ... le duc p les
mamo dud villes vny ... belle ... riche grant croix dor ... darnes apperte
a joellin mon ... le duc la quelle ... en deus pretes dont une de oro dont
pretes fait la croix ... une vny ... pre sur la ... se port lad croix garnie
joelle croix de ... beaulx grosso saphirs de ... beaulx grosso balais
de emgnar belles grosso ples ... de trois dyamans pointuz ... les
les clony du armesiones ... ya ... mijcloz les ... vornes delad croix
... me dame ... sent jeha a demp les ... en bas bon dicelle croix une
reliquiaire en ... due des pontes de senn ... georne ... est ... pre ...
vno ... mage de me ... en vny tombean de cristal garny a l'enron
led ... saphirs ... balais ... pres ... ya trois ... ... de home
darnes denar led tombean ... sur joellin vny angle ... est le hault
dicellen pre ... saffror led croix en maniere dune montaigne esmaille
de vero ... est joellin croix en deus estmis de omr la quelle croix mond
led duc a san baille aud bokeland jo ... la luy garder En tesmoing de
ce a ceste parces dendenture demon ... deus led villes led bokeland
a mis son signet ... signe manuel lan ... jo ... deffusd ... signe
richart bokeland

Ault copie

Ceste endenture fait a calais le ... jo danst lan m ... cccc ... eno
puissat prince mon ... le roynal ... regent le Royaume de france ...
duc de bedford dune part ... villes de ferrers secretaire de garde
de coffres prines dud ... dant ... tesmoing ... led villes por ce on nom
de mond ... le royet ... de son comandemer a baille ... delivre led jo

between Normandy and Brittany. The conquest of Maine and Anjou now seemed certain. The following year, in August 1425, Richard Beauchamp, Earl of Warwick took Le Mans, capital of Maine.

The French war effort remained paralysed and it seemed as if the English were poised to seize a whole swathe of territory linking Gascony in the south to Normandy in the north. Bedford's absence in England from 1425–27 did not hinder the English war effort in the slightest. He returned to France in 1427 with a freshly raised army and, together with new levies of English-born soldiers from Normandy, a new offensive was launched.

THE SIEGE OF ORLÉANS TO THE SIEGE OF CALAIS, 1428–36

This campaign culminated in the siege of Orléans. At the same time it signalled the end of English successes. The siege began in October 1428 but quickly turned sour. The death in November of Salisbury, the English commander, was a major blow to English morale. This, coupled with the sudden explosion on to the scene of Joan of Arc, the Maid of Orléans, gave the French fresh heart. Under her leadership the siege was raised. Events turned from bad to worse for the English. On 18 June 1429 an army under Lord Scales, the Earl of Shrewsbury and Sir John Fastolf suffered a crushing defeat at Patay in the Loire Valley.

These successes allowed the French to seize the military initiative for the first time in 20 years. A month later, on 18 July, the Dauphin was crowned Charles VII with the sacred oil of the ancient Merovingian King, Clovis, in the cathedral at Rheims. Joan

John, Duke of Bedford kneeling before St George. The saint is dressed in the ermine-lined sovereign's robe of the Order of the Garter over full armour, and attended by a squire carrying his helmet, shield and lance. Bedford was committed to upholding the values of the Order and its chivalric code. He was appointed Regent of France, according to the wishes of Henry V, during the minority of the infant Henry VI.

Joan of Arc announcing the liberation of Orléans to Charles VII. Although Joan was not the commander of the army that was gathered to relieve the city, which had been under siege since October 1428, her presence inspired the soldiers with confidence. After entering the city with supplies, Joan led a series of sallies against the English, forcing them to withdraw in early May 1429. Joan left Orléans on May 9 and met Charles at Tours where she urged him to make haste to Rheims to be crowned.

of Arc was captured by the Burgundians at Compiègne on 23 May 1430. She was handed over to the English at Rouen, condemned as a heretic and burnt at the stake in May 1431. Yet even this success did little to boost the confidence of the English.

To prevent this sudden collapse in confidence spreading further, a major counterstroke was required. At Bedford's urging it was decided to bring forward the coronation of Henry VI. A ceremony was conducted at Westminster Abbey in November 1429, designed to reflect his status as the first king of two realms. Plans were then made for another coronation to be held in France. Henry VI was finally escorted over to France in 1430. He landed at Calais on St George's Day 1430 but because of French domination of Champagne and the Oise Valley it was not judged safe enough to bring him to Paris until December 1431. With an entourage of several thousands, he entered the city on 2 December. In a ceremony that

French chroniclers recorded as particularly English, Henry was crowned King of France on 16 December. By 29 January 1432 he was back in England, never again to return to his French realm.

Declining military fortunes and the failure of periodic peace negotiations now resulted in disagreements on how the war should be conducted. Bedford's principal concern was the defence of Normandy. He was content to leave Paris and territory to the east and south to the Burgundians. Stung by criticism from his brother, Gloucester, who favoured a more rigorous defence of Calais rather than Normandy, he returned to England in 1433 and submitted a plan to the Council to secure the finance necessary to create a permanent field army in Normandy. This had the potential to secure the long-term security of the Duchy. Little came of these plans.

Bedford returned to Normandy in 1434. His death in September 1435 was another blow to English morale. He had tried to remain true to the wishes of his brother and defend the newly won possessions. His death robbed the English of strong, experienced leadership. Moreover, it now emerged that at the recent Congress of Arras in August 1435, where peace negotiations between England, France and Burgundy were conducted, Philip, Duke of Burgundy had made peace with Charles VII. As a result the conference collapsed and the French resumed operations against English-held territory. See document 18, *Papal intervention in France*.

In April 1436 Paris fell to Charles VII. Shortly afterwards, in July, the Burgundians attacked Calais. The fall of Paris had been expected. The attack on Calais generated much more concern. Its defence was vital,

Portrait of Philip the Good, Duke of Burgundy wearing the collar of the chivalric Order of the Golden Fleece. The Duke founded the Order in 1430 and it became one of the leading chivalric orders in Christendom. Although initially supporting the English after the assassination of his father, Duke Philip made his peace with Charles VII in 1435 and thereafter trod a cautious path in his relations with both countries.

18 *Papal intervention in France*

A Papal Bull confirming that French nobles had not been released from their oaths of loyalty to Henry V and Henry VI, 17 August 1435.

The last decades of the fourteenth century had witnessed the Great Schism in the Catholic Church. A disputed papal election in 1378 resulted in two rival popes: one based at Rome; the other at Avignon in the south of France. Until then English policy had been simple: to support that pope opposed to the French-backed candidate. However, the Great Schism came to an end in 1417 when Martin V was elected with the authority of the Council of Constance.

Henry V clearly wished to gain papal approval for his ambitions in France.

Martin V, on the other hand, wished to restore the much diminished prestige of the papacy and reassert his authority in England. Whilst the King and Pope disagreed over papal authority in England – Henry refused to allow his kinsman Henry Beaufort to take up his position as a cardinal in 1418 – there was never any serious confrontation. Moreover, Henry allowed Martin V to appoint bishops in Normandy without any hindrance. Despite this concession, Martin V never actually recognized the Treaty of Troyes or Henry V as Regent of France.

During Henry VI's minority Anglo–Papal relations remained stable. Martin V continued with his efforts to increase ecclesiastical authority in England. The Duke of Bedford tried hard to win the Pope's backing and assistance in Normandy. Pope Eugenius IV succeeded Martin V in 1431 and undertook to mediate between the French and English to bring about a peaceful solution to the conflict. Papal negotiators were active at the Congress of Arras in 1435. Unfortunately the only substantial outcome of that set of negotiations was an alliance between Philip, Duke of Burgundy and Charles VII of France. Despite these papal initiatives, Eugenius IV still found time to issue a Papal Bull confirming that he had not released those French princes and nobles who had sworn oaths of loyalty to Henry V and Henry VI from their promises.

THE PAPAL BULL READS:

Eugenius, bishop, servant of the servants of God, to his most dear son in Christ, Henry, illustrious King of England, greetings and apostolic blessings. Our beloved son Adam Moleyns, your envoy and orator, has delivered to us your letter, entrusted to him by your highness and prudently disclosed to those in attendance with him, your faithful subjects and our venerable brother and beloved son, the bishop of Amiens and Andrew Holeys, our refendary and chamberlain, which we have heard with pleasure and have graciously responded to point by point. However, since you wished to be informed by us of releases from oaths sworn by some of the princes and nobility of France, being of sound mind, to your father and to yourself, namely whether they have sought them, and whether we have granted what has been sought by them or in their name, we inform your highness that we have absolved no-one from such oaths, nor has there been any entreaty to us by them or in their name for any such absolutions. In future, however, you should trust that in this matter and in all others bearing upon your honour and desire that you should rightly remain content concerning ourself. We therefore, with as much affection as we may, urge and press upon your excellency, whom we acknowledge to be well disposed towards the good of peace, to be daily better disposed towards an end finally being brought to so great a calamity, within your life-time and mine, so that, abandoning your warlike intent and zeal, which are displeasing to God, your soul and spirit might be turned towards the pious counsels of salvation, winning great merit with God, who rewards such good works, the most gracious benevolence from ourself and the greatest glory among men of this world and the universal orb of perpetual renown.

Florence in the year of Dominical Incarnation 1435, 17th August in the fifth year of our pontificate.
John de Manciochis.

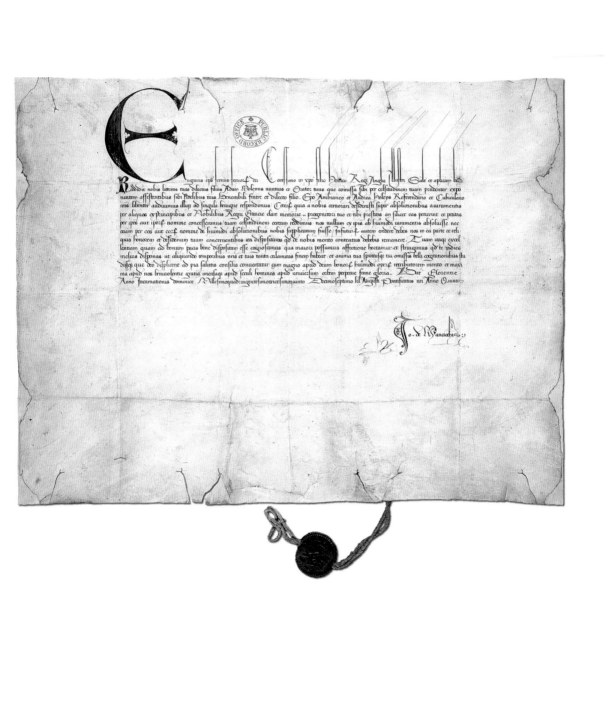

not only from a financial perspective, but also for reasons of national prestige. Fortunately, divisions amongst the Burgundians led to the siege being abandoned after three weeks.

CONQUEST OR NEGOTIATION:
THE SEARCH FOR A SOLUTION, 1436–45

It had become more than apparent by now that Henry VI did not have the personality or intelligence of his father. For a while Bedford had held the English war effort together. His loss had robbed the English of their most experienced commander in Normandy. With Henry VI failing to demonstrate any warlike characteristics, it was necessary to find a leader with sufficient vigour to direct affairs in France. During Richard, Duke of York's brief appointment as Lieutenant, Pontoise was taken in February 1437. However, York was replaced by the more experienced Richard Beauchamp, Earl of Warwick that year. Although not of the blood-royal, Warwick was one of the foremost warriors of the age. Yet Warwick died in 1439. After some hesitation York was again appointed Lieutenant of France in 1440, proving acceptable to both Gloucester and Beaufort, as well as Bedford's former supporters in the Duchy.

A new peace conference was held at Gravelines in the summer of 1439. Little of substance was achieved because each side proved unwilling to modify its demands. The only tangible outcome was the release of the Duke of Orléans, a prisoner since Agincourt. In an uncharacteristic show of determination, Henry VI pushed through his release, very much against the advice of Gloucester who thought this would only serve to strengthen the French position.

The continuing failure of peace negotiations between 1440 and 1443 resulted in a shift in policy back to one of conquest. Despite the questionable state of English finances, a cause of increasing concern after the late 1430s, it was decided that a determined effort would be made to conquer the area between

Charles, Duke of Orléans shown imprisoned in the Tower of London. He was captured at the battle of Agincourt in 1415, taken to England and imprisoned in the Tower where a ransom of 300,000 crowns was placed on his head. Charles remained in the Tower for 25 years, writing poetry in French and English. He was released in 1440, against the advice of the Duke of Gloucester, in the hope that he could help advance the peace process between the English and French.

Normandy and Gascony, despite the shortage of available funds. Concerns about the security of Gascony were being voiced more frequently. A combination of French attacks and defections amongst the Gascon nobility had caused considerable anxiety in a previously secure part of the English patrimony. See document 19, *Rewarding a Gascon supporter*.

A more aggressive English stance was thus designed to halt this gradual erosion of territory. The King's cousin, John Beaufort, Duke of Somerset was placed in charge of the operation. He was appointed captain and governor of Anjou and Maine. This caused some confusion within the English chain of command. It was unclear how his authority related to that of York as Lieutenant of France. In the event, the operation proved to be an unmitigated

Grant of the castle at Sarnesio to François de Montferant, knight, 22 March 1437.

As part of the ancient patrimony of the kings of England, the security of Gascony was the responsibility of Englishmen. After the deaths of Henry V and Charles VI in 1422, the minority Council in England thought Gascony could provide an ideal springboard from which to launch the conquest of those parts of France that had yet to acknowledge Henry VI as successor to the joint-monarchy.

However, the weakened state of the Duchy, financially and militarily, meant that this was unachievable during the 1420s, especially when resources intended for that theatre of operations were often diverted elsewhere. Indeed, in 1429 an army intended for Sir John Radcliffe, Seneschal of Gascony, was instead employed in the north of the realm.

The King's Council therefore came to rely on other French lords and captains to protect the Duchy to a greater extent than before. Financial inducements and other rewards were distributed to key supporters there. The Montferant family was one of the leading baronial families in Gascony, and its fortunes had been intimately tied to those of the English Crown for centuries. Indeed, French chroniclers regarded its members as the most hardened Anglophiles in the region. It was therefore in the interests of the Crown to maintain the support of this family.

One such instance is the reward to Sir François de Montferant for his services in 1437. This was done in recognition of his activities at the 'New Castle' at Sarnesio. The castle had been granted to Gaston de Foix, Count of Longueville before it had actually been taken from the King's enemies. It was Montferant who personally took control of the operation and seized the castle with the aid of a considerable quantity of cannons. During the assault the castle took a considerable battering and part of its defences collapsed. For his diligent service Montferant was given custody of the castle. The Montferants remained one of the mainstays of the administration in Gascony until its final loss to Charles VII in 1453.

THE GRANT READS:

To all to whom these come, etc, greetings. Know that whereas lately certain lords of our Duchy of Aquitaine, specifically our dear and faithful Gaston de Foix, Count of Longueville, the Lord of Montferant and François de Montferant, knight, and also other of our subjects of our city of Bordeaux has besieged and transferred to our obedience the New Castle in Sarnesio; yet before the surrender it was agreed between them that once the said place had been taken and recovered, it should be placed and remain in the possession and custody of the said Lord of Montferant by French copyhold and assigned for his annual wages; after which the said Lord of Montferant was unable to attend to the custody of the said place, the said Francis, at the request of the same Lord of Montferant took the burden upon himself, and the same place, during the siege was broken by cannons and engines and a great part of its walls fell to the earth, so that not it could not now be defended against our enemies; whereupon the said Francis having undertaken not inconsiderable repairs and incurred substantial expenses, held a great part of the people there for its security, seeing that he would not have any wages or reward on this account, as he maintains.

We, considering these matters and the good and faithful service given to us and which will be given by the said Francis both in the act of war and in other ways, have of our special grace granted and conceded to him that by force of these present letters, he might have, hold and defend in the form in which he has held it since the said surrender and now holds until he or those, who by our special gift or by other means, might wish to have that place, have made to him full satisfaction and payment of his said wages and everything they know (or might have known) that he had duly and faithfully done and spent by way of the aforesaid repairs. In which things, etc, Testified by the King at the manor of Lambeth, 22 March. By writ of privy seal.

Dum... ad pacem pro satim. Pactis vero cum leone de Nono castro in carnesio nup[er] p[er] quondam ... ducatus n[ost]r[i] Aquitan[ie] ... spalie p[ro] dilec[t]o et fidele n[ost]ro Easton de ffosp comitem de longcastr ... d[omi]n[u]m de mountfort et ffranciscum de mountfort militem n[ost]r[u]m ... alio m[od]o sub[d]itos committens ... custodie in ... dedic[i]r[u]m p[er] obsidionem posit[us] fuisset et reddit[us] ante annum reddicionem eadem approximatum fuisset me d[i]c[t]o d[i]c[t]o ... d[i]c[t]o loco capto et intempto p[er] ... pendit et remanet in manibz et in custodia p[re]d[i]c[t]a d[omi]n[u]m de mountfort et p[re]sentis ffranc[i]e sibi p[er] vad[i]is ... assignatis ... ... postea d[i]c[t]o d[i]c[t]o de mountfort custodie d[i]c[t]a loca vacare non potuisse ... ffranascius ad requisicionem eiusdem d[omi]n[i] de mountfort omne onus de suscepit idemq[ue] leone d[i]c[t]o obsidionis duravere stat[us] fuit p[er] canones et ingenia et magna parte minori eiusdem ad ... p[er]tit ... nullo modo erat defensabilis ad resistend[um] nimias n[ost]r[as] ... q[ue]n[m] p[re]d[i]c[t]us ffranascius ... c[on]tente non modicus omnat[us] et expensas in eodem ... exit ... ad magnam partem genorum p[er] comp[u]tam sua ibidem remisit absq[ue] hoc q[ue] ipse cogn[ovi]t de nob[is] ex hac causa aliqua vad[i]a seu p[ro]p[ri]et[a]te hinc ... ... Nos p[re]missa considerantes ac bona et fidelia servic[ia] nob[is] p[er] p[re]d[i]c[t]um ffranciscum impensa et impendend[a] tam in ... grosso qu[m] alie de gr[ati]a n[ost]ra sp[eci]ali dedim[us] et concessim[us] ei q[uo]d ipse ... p[re]sentem d[i]c[t]um locum de stono castro hoie teneo et custodia posset in forma q[am] ipse tenuit a d[i]c[t]o ... et tenet de ... quousq[ue] illo vel illi qui p[er] donacionem n[ost]ram aut alio m[od]o locum illam ... possunt vel potuit sibi fecint vel fecit int[eg]ram satisfaccion[em] et allocacem eor[um] vad[i]or[um] ... de omni eo q[uo]d ipse conuit aut potit a debito et fideli ratione reparavit ac recepit feasse et expendisse. In cui[us] &c. T[este] R[ege] apud Manno de lamehirch xxvj die majo

T[este] ... de privato sigillo.

... d[i]c[us] et Duram[us] ... ... solut ... ... Robert et ... ...

disaster. Somerset had been captured at the English defeat at Baugé in 1421 and not released until 1438. His experiences had made him a bitter man. In fact, his principal consideration seemed to be to make a personal profit. Somerset landed in Normandy in August 1443 but failed to make any significant territorial gains. He subsequently returned to England in disgrace, accused of incompetence and attacking the territory of one of England's allies, the Duke of Brittany. He died in May 1444. Rumours pointed to suicide as the cause.

Portrait of Charles VII, wearing a hat with an unusual zig-zag design, and a richly decorated collar. Although removed from the succession under the terms of the Treaty of Troyes in 1420, Charles continued to resist the English. The power and prestige of the French monarchy revived during the 1430s. It was during his reign that important financial and military reforms took place which facilitated the final defeat of the English in France.

In the wake of Somerset's farcical expedition, a new initiative for peace began in 1443 with the offer of a French bride for Henry VI. The choice of Margaret, daughter of Réné, Duke of Anjou and titular King of Jerusalem, suited Charles VII more than the English. The French King wished to recover Maine, the most recent and strongly held English conquest. With Maine safe, the English would finally have to abandon hopes of securing Anjou. Charles VII could therefore attack Normandy if he chose.

THE LOSS OF LANCASTRIAN FRANCE, 1445–50

Despite some reservations, the decision to negotiate with the French was taken. Talks were conducted at Tours in 1444 by the Earl of Suffolk, an experienced veteran of the wars until the early 1430s. It seems likely that Suffolk indicated a willingness to surrender Maine in return for securing Gascony and Normandy in full sovereignty. If accepted, Henry VI would then abandon his claim to the French throne. However, the French would only move on the marriage of Henry and Margaret. Despite this, a marriage treaty was still concluded along with a 21-month truce. Margaret's dower was to consist of her mother's empty claims to the Kingdom of Majorca and 20,000 francs.

Although the surrender of Maine had been agreed, achieving this proved difficult. Further extensions of the truce were to become conditional upon it being handed over. In July 1445 the French sent an embassy to England led by Charles VII's kinsman, Louis, Prince of Bourbon. The French were no longer prepared to include Normandy in any discussions. They were only willing to offer Gascony and Calais in full sovereignty. Despite this stance Henry VI gave a solemn undertaking to surrender Maine before 1 October 1445 to the departing embassy.

Attempting to implement this agreement dominated English policy for the following two years. A mixture of delays and prevarication dogged any final settlement. In December 1446 Edmund Beaufort, Marquess of Dorset, younger brother of John Beaufort, Duke of Somerset was appointed Lieutenant of France, presumably in the hope that he would surrender Maine which had been granted to him by his uncle, Bedford. Dorset, created Duke of Somerset in 1448, had enjoyed a successful military career in France, distinguishing himself on a number of occasions, including the siege and capture of Harfleur in 1440.

It was finally agreed that Maine would be surrendered on 1 November 1447. On 28 July 1447 the English captains Matthew Gough and Fulk Eyton were ordered to receive Maine from Edmund Beaufort. In his capacity as Lieutenant of France he was also directed to provide soldiers to help enforce the surrender. His officers, Sir Osbert Mountford and Sir Richard Frogenhall, refused to comply and employed a number of delaying tactics, including demands for compensation for those about to be dispossessed. This situation dragged on into 1448, causing considerable anger amongst the French, who accused Gough of being in league with Somerset's officers.

In the meantime Charles VII mobilized his troops with the intention of commencing hostilities. His army surrounded Le Mans in February 1448 with approximately 6–7,000 troops. The English numbered about 2,000, reinforced from Normandy by Roger, Lord Camoys. During the course of the siege there were several violent skirmishes. After emergency negotiations the Treaty of Lavardin was agreed on 11 March 1448, by which the surrender of Maine was agreed once again.

In March 1448 Somerset finally arrived in Normandy to take up his office. The Duchy was increasingly unstable. The English and French repeatedly accused each other of deliberately inciting trouble. English relations with Brittany had also deteriorated and the Duke had even performed homage for those lands he held from Charles VII. Brittany now replaced Maine as the principal English strategic concern. In March 1449, the seizure of Fougères on the Breton–Norman frontier by François de Surienne, an Aragonese knight in English service, alienated the Bretons and provided the French with an excuse to renew hostilities against the English, who had clearly violated the truce.

The military recovery of Normandy by French and Breton forces proceeded with lightening speed. Rouen, the capital of the Duchy, surrendered in October 1449. In a last-ditch attempt to shore up the English position, Sir Thomas Kyriell was sent with an army of 4,500 men in December 1449. The battle of Formigny of 15 April 1450 signalled the collapse of the English power in the Duchy of

The defeat of the English army, led by Sir Thomas Kyriell at the battle of Formigny on 15 April 1450, signalled the complete disintegration of their power in the Duchy of Normandy. The English, shown huddled together on the right-hand side, are attempting to defend themselves with lances, and supported by archers, against the massed ranks of the charging French knights.

Mounted French knights carrying fleur-de-lys banners shown entering Bordeaux in triumph in 1451. The loss of Bordeaux spelt the effective end of English rule in its ancient Duchy of Gascony. One final attempt was made to recover the Duchy in 1453. However, the defeat of the expeditionary force, under the command of the Earl of Shrewsbury at the battle of Castillon on 17 July, dashed any remaining hope of recovering England's long-standing French possession.

Normandy. Kyriell was captured along with a number of leading captains. The remaining English garrisons had fallen by August 1450. The fall of Cherbourg on 12 August that year meant that the reconquest had taken little more than a year. See the loss of Normandy: document 20, *The disaster at Formigny*.

In the south of France, Gascony had also been rapidly over-whelmed. The loss of Bordeaux in 1451 spelt the effective end of English rule in its ancient Duchy there. One final attempt was made to recover Gascony. At the battle of Castillon on 17 July 1453 the English expeditionary force was dramatically defeated and the Earl of Shrewsbury, one of England's foremost warriors, slain on the field. The only English possession remaining in France was now the town of Calais. England was never to achieve such a dominant position in France as it had done under Henry V.

A petition to allow the gathering of alms to pay for a ransom of English prisoners captured at the battle of Formigny, *c.* 1450–53.

Apart from loss of life or crippling injury, one of the pitfalls of fighting on the losing side in a battle was the possibility of capture by the enemy and being put to ransom. The Crown rarely came to the aid of those held to ransom, even for their leading nobles. The Duke of Orléans languished in England for 25 years after his capture at Agincourt. John Beaufort, Duke of Somerset found himself in captivity in France for 17 years after his capture at Bagué in 1421. For the majority of captives it was necessary to seek the assistance of family and friends back in England. The petition by Thomas Sewstern of Lincolnshire is a typical example of the difficulties involved for a relatively unimportant man-at-arms without apparent access to patronage in securing his release.

Sewstern brought a suit into Chancery asking to be allowed to gather alms throughout England to help pay the ransoms of John Swan and John Hayward. Swan and Hayward, possibly former brothers-in-arms, had been captured after Sir Thomas Kyriell's defeat at the battle of Formigny in 1450. Kyriell was a leading veteran of the French wars and had been sent to Normandy with a force to relieve its beleaguered garrisons in the Duchy. His army had been intercepted at Formigny by a French army commanded by the Count of Clerment. The outcome remained uncertain until a second French army commanded by the Counts of Richemont and Laval arrived. Formigny was a military disaster for the English and effectively spelt the end of Lancastrian France. One dejected English estimate put the total captured at 900 and their dead at over 2,000.

After a long spell in prison, Swan had been put to ransom for the sum of one mark (13 shillings and 4 pence) and 6 scarlet hats. John Hayward had been put to ransom for the sum of 26 salutes (a gold coin first struck by Charles VI of France). Swan and Hayward, it would appear, only had their friendship with Sewstern to fall back upon. Sewstern was not a wealthy man, however, and was forced to make an appeal for a grant of letters patent to be able to collect donations wherever he could find them. If the ransoms were not paid, he asserted, Swan would have to swear allegiance to France or be executed. As with so many of these cases, the final outcome is unknown.

THE PETITION READS:

Beseeching right meekly Thomas Sewstern of Sewstern in the County of Lincoln. That whereas one John Swan of the said town at the time of the distressing of Sir Thomas Kyriell was taken prisoner at Formigny in Normandy brought to Carington, there being in dure prison [i.e., a long time in prison] put to fine and ransom of a mark of silver and vi bonnets of scarlet. And also is pledged for one John Hayward for xxvi salutes abiding in England and not returned there again for to pay his ransom. And unless the finances of the said John Swan and John Hayward be paid and content by the Feast of Pentecost now next following else the said John Swan must needs be sworn French or utterly die. That it may please your Reverend Fatherhood and Gracious Lordship to grant to the said beseecher letters patent of our Sovereign Lord the King for to endure by a whole year by virtue of the which he may gather alms through the realm of England to content the said ransoms at Reverence of God and in way of charity.

The Enduring
Reputation of Henry V

Henry V has continued to fascinate the English ever since his victory at Agincourt in 1415. Not surprisingly, the memory of Henry and his achievements was to be called upon at those moments when the English cause in France was faltering during the reign of his ineffectual son, Henry VI.

This reputation continued to inspire Englishmen in the sixteenth century. The glorious events of Henry V's reign were twice invoked by Henry VIII: first, when he invaded France in 1513; and second, in the 1530s, when this Tudor monarch was trying to stir up patriotic feelings against the Pope.

Laurence Olivier shown as Henry V leading his army to victory at the battle of Agincourt in 1415. Olivier was both star and director in this adaptation of Shakespeare's *Henry V*. It was both a triumph of modern cinema and an unashamedly nationalistic portrayal of the courage and bravery of the British character in times of adversity. It has set the tone for the public's perception of Henry V ever since.

The presentation of Henry V's exploits to a wider audience reached a degree of maturity in the work of the sixteenth-century chroniclers, Raphael Holinshed and Edward Hall. Indeed, Shakespeare borrowed heavily from Holinshed when writing his own play for Elizabethan audiences. Shakespeare was very much concerned with creating a figure who could be admired not merely for his personal qualities, but also for what he was able to do for the benefit of the country he ruled.

There can be no surprise that Henry's achievements lived on into the twentieth century through the creation of Shakespeare's hero. The advent of cinema did much for this appeal. Film critics stated that Laurence Olivier took his adaptation of the play, *Henry V*, to unprecedented heights for the cinema. When James Agee reviewed

the film for *Time* magazine on 8 April 1946 he claimed that: 'The movies have produced one of their rare great works of art.'

This was a film as important for its celebration of Britain and its people in adverse times, as for its approach to the play itself. It was a very self-conscious attempt to depict the strength of the British character for explicitly propagandist purposes, entirely in keeping with the intentions of Henry's earlier biographers. Shakespeare had written his play when England was under threat from Spain. Olivier's adaptation, although coming too late in the Second

An engraving showing the three kings of the Lancastrian dynasty. On the left is Henry IV, the founder of the dynasty who deposed Richard II in 1399; in the centre is Henry V who achieved brilliant military success in France; and on the right

World War to act as a call to arms, nonetheless acted as a powerful reminder of a Britain under siege from an external enemy.

Given Henry V's reputation down the centuries, it is unavoidable that a study of his reign should focus on his career as a warrior. Henry was a man of action with strongly held convictions. He had a forceful and energetic character, first employed in the Welsh campaigns against Glyndwr. These qualities gave rise to some frustration when not deployed. It is perhaps within this context that we should interpret the unlikely stories surrounding his youth and the more believable clashes between father and son towards the end of Henry IV's reign.

is the weak and ineffectual Henry VI whose reign saw English power in France collapse completely by 1450. The depiction of Henry V is the same as that which appears on the miniature of Henry V by Bernard Lens at the front of this book.

Once King, Henry was freed from the limitations that had been imposed upon him. He was now able to show what he was made of. Convinced of the righteousness of his cause against the French, he put the country on a war-footing, and set in motion a chain of events which would see England gain military and political dominance over much of the Kingdom of France. In achieving this, Henry V restored English national pride and gave the English a hero to be proud of.

Who's Who

Thomas Arundel, Archbishop of Canterbury, 1353–1414 Youngest son of the Earl of Arundel. After attending Oxford University, he was appointed Bishop of Ely in 1373 at the age of 20. He became identified with the baronial opposition to Richard II from 1386. This led to his temporary promotion to Archbishop of York and Chancellor of England in 1388. Dismissed in 1389 he was re-appointed Chancellor in 1391. He resigned as Chancellor in 1396 when he became Archbishop of Canterbury. Like other opponents of Richard II, Arundel was dismissed in 1397. He was moved to the see of St Andrews and banished abroad. Whilst in exile he joined the opposition forming around Henry Boling-broke. Following his accession as Henry IV, Arundel was re-appointed Archbishop of Canter-bury. As Henry IV's health declined Arundel became the dominant royal councillor, serving twice more as Chancellor. This led to conflict with Prince Henry who assumed a leading role in government between 1409–11. Prince Henry was outmanoeuvred, however, and the King reasserted control of government until his death in 1413.

Edmund Beaufort, Duke of Somerset, *c.* 1406–55 As grandson of John of Gaunt, Somerset was at the very centre of the Lancastrian regime. He inherited his title in 1444, but diligent service in France from the 1420s had already given him major lands and offices in England's French possessions. In 1446 he became commander-in-chief in France, but his poor leadership allowed a sapping of English morale just as the French rallied. He oversaw the final English expulsion from France.

When Henry VI's government began to experience financial difficulties Somerset found his own resources pressurized. Somerset's conduct in France undermined his reputation and he clung to the court faction of William, Duke of Suffolk. This, and the failure of his military leadership, made him a focus for Richard, Duke of York's hostility. Henry VI did little to end royal favour towards Somerset, restoring him to favour after his bouts of insanity. This contributed towards the polarization of political factions. Somerset was killed fighting against Richard, Duke of York at the first battle of St Albans in 1455.

Henry Beaufort, Bishop of Winchester, 1376–1447 The second son of John of Gaunt, Duke of Lancaster by his mistress, Katherine Swynford. He attended Cambridge and Oxford Universities. In 1398 he was appointed Bishop of Lincoln before moving to the richest bishopric in the country, Winchester, in 1404 which he held for 43 years.

Beaufort was an able administrator, diplomat and royal councillor. During his first term as Chancellor in 1403–1405 he backed Prince Henry's policies. He was made Chancellor under the new King from 1413–17 and whole-heartedly supported the King's venture against the 'ancient enemy'. In 1417 Beaufort was created a Cardinal and Papal Legate by Pope Martin V. Henry V would not allow him to accept that dignity until 1421.

Beaufort was one of the leading politicians during the minority of Henry VI but was frequently in conflict with the new King's uncle, Humphrey, Duke of Gloucester. The financial support Beaufort was able to provide to the Crown was indispensable to the English war-effort. Beaufort's influence at Court waned during the 1440s as he was supplanted by a younger generation of politicians.

John, Duke of Bedford, 1389–1435 Third son of Henry IV, he ruled Lancastrian France for Henry VI from 1422–35. He was a successful soldier, diplomat and statesman. Bedford had acquired substantial military experience during his life, long before his creation as Duke in

1414. He served as warden of the East March against Scotland from 1403–14. His appointment as Guardian of England from 1415–21 meant that he missed the battle of Agincourt. After the death of Henry V he became Regent of France until Henry VI's coronation in 1431. Thereafter he became the King's Lieutenant in France but continued to remain in charge of the war-effort. Affairs in England were left primarily in the hands of his younger brother, Humphrey, Duke of Gloucester.

Bedford saw it as his duty to continue the conquest of France in line with his brother's wishes. English successes continued until 1429 when, at the siege of Orléans, Joan of Arc inspired the French forces. The English abandoned the siege and for the next 20 years fought a defensive war. When Bedford died in 1435, however, the English still possessed more French territory than they had done on the death of Henry V.

John, Duke of Burgundy 'The Fearless', 1371–1419 The son of Philip the Bold, Duke of Burgundy, and Margaret of Flanders, he earned his nickname, 'The Fearless' after the disastrous defeat of a western crusading army by the Turks at Nicopolis in Greece. In 1396 John succeeded his father. His rivalry with his first cousin, the King's younger brother, Louis, Duke of Orléans, helped to provoke civil war in France. Each man sought control of Charles VI and Paris. Whilst the assassination by Duke John of his cousin in 1407 enabled him to subdue Paris and the Crown, the opposition to the Burgundians by Louis's followers and heirs, known as the Armagnacs, continued.

After Henry V's invasion, Duke John conducted intermittent negotiations with the King, although this did not lead to a firm Anglo–Burgundian alliance. In the autumn of 1419 John turned to the Armagnacs in the hope of arranging a truce or even a firm peace settlement. The two princes met on the bridge of Montereau. However, Duke John was struck down and killed during a dispute started by the Armagnacs, a political assassination that was almost certainly premeditated.

Philip, Duke of Burgundy 'The Good', 1419–67 Son of Duke John 'The Fearless'. After his father was murdered in 1419, Philip formed an alliance with King Henry V of England. Under the Treaty of Troyes in 1420, Philip recognized Henry V as heir to the French throne; the Dauphin was disinherited. Philip aided the efforts of Henry and his successor to establish English rule in France. Finally, in return for important concessions, Philip ended the English alliance and made peace with Charles VII in the Treaty of Arras in 1435.

Despite the truce, Philip's relations with Charles were not always amicable. In 1440 he temporarily supported the rebellious nobles against the King and gave asylum to the Dauphin, later Louis XI, who was constantly in revolt against his father. In 1463, Philip was forced to return some of his lands to Louis XI. He was succeeded by his ambitious son, Charles the Bold, who took control of the government from Philip in 1465.

Thomas, Lord Camoys, c.? –1421 Camoys was probably the half-nephew of Thomas, Lord Camoys (d. 1372), succeeding to the family estates in 1372. By 1383 he was a knight banneret, a clear indication of his martial interests. Although identified as one of Richard II's favourites, he transferred without problem into the service of the Lancastrians and enjoyed an active military and diplomatic career under Henry IV and Henry V. In 1400 he served against Glyndwr's rebels in Wales, whilst in 1403 he conducted Princess Joan from Brittany to England for her marriage to the King. His principal achievement, however, was commanding the left wing of the English army at Agincourt on 25 October 1415. In 1416 he was made a Knight of the Garter. Camoys married firstly, Elizabeth, daughter of William Louches and secondly, Elizabeth, widow of Sir Henry Percy ('Hotspur'). He died on 28 March 1421.

Charles VII, 1403–61 Born in Paris, Charles was the eldest surviving son of Charles VI of France and Isabeau de Bavière. On the death of his father in 1422, the French throne did not pass to Charles but to his infant nephew, King Henry VI of England in accordance with his father's Treaty of Troyes of 1420, designed to end the Anglo–French conflict.

Without any organized French army, the English strengthened their grip over France until 8 March 1429 when Joan of Arc, claiming divine inspiration, urged Charles to declare himself King and raise an army to liberate France from the English. One of the important factors that aided in the ultimate success of Charles VII was support from the family of his wife Marie d'Anjou. After the French victory at the battle of Patay, Charles was crowned Charles VII of France on 17 July 1429, in Rheims Cathedral. Charles VII then recaptured Paris from the English, and eventually all of France, with the exception of the northern port of Calais. He died on 22 July 1461 at Mehun-sur-Yèvre, although his latter years were marked by an open revolt by his son who succeeded him as Louis XI.

Humphrey, Duke of Gloucester, 1390–1447 Youngest brother of Henry V, Gloucester was recognized by contemporaries as handsome and well-mannered, kind and generous, brave and pious. However, he was also impatient, reckless, inflexible and arrogant. For this reason he was not given command of the war-effort in France. By the terms of his will, Henry V wished him to govern England, although the precise

arrangements were unclear. Gloucester claimed the Regency but the minority Council and Parliament would only confirm him as Protector and Defender of England. Gloucester resented these restrictions and blamed Cardinal Beaufort.

Gloucester's power was probably at its peak in 1432–33 when he managed to purge the royal household and install his own men. Following the death of Bedford in 1435 Gloucester became heir apparent, but the King preferred his Beaufort kinsmen and Gloucester's influence steadily declined. His position deteriorated further after the arrest and trial of his second wife, Eleanor Cobham, on charges of sorcery and necromancy. In 1441 Eleanor was sentenced to life imprisonment where she remained until her death in 1454. The shame and humiliation only hastened Gloucester's demise. In February 1447 he was arrested and died in mysterious circumstances in his lodgings.

Owain Glyndwr, *c.* 1354– *c.* 1416 A descendant of the princes of Powys, Glyndwr inherited several manors in northern Wales. He studied law in London and then served with the forces of Henry Bolingbroke, later King Henry IV. In September 1400, a year after Bolingbroke usurped the throne, Glyndwr's violent feud with a neighbour, Lord Grey of Ruthin, touched off an uprising in northern Wales which spread across the Principality. Glyndwr formed an alliance with Henry's most powerful opponents, and by 1404 he had control of most of Wales. Styling himself Prince of Wales, he established an independent Welsh Parliament and even began to formulate his own foreign and ecclesiastical policies. In 1405, he was twice defeated by Henry IV's son, Prince Henry, and his allies in England were crushed. Reinforcements sent by France could not save his cause. By 1408–1409 Prince Henry had captured Glyndwr's main strongholds, but the rebel was active in guerrilla fighting as late as 1412.

Henry IV, 1366–1413 Born at Bolingbroke in Lincolnshire. The eldest son of John of Gaunt, Duke of Lancaster by his first wife Blanche, daughter and heiress of Henry, Duke of Lancaster. Created Earl of Derby in 1377. He married Mary de Bohun, daughter and co-heiress of Humphrey, Earl of Hereford, Essex and Northampton in 1380.

Created Duke of Hereford in 1397, Bolingbroke became involved with the noble opposition to Richard II, but was lucky to escape serious retribution after his father, John of Gaunt's intervention. Initially exiled for ten years, he was then sentenced to permanent exile and his inheritance confiscated after Gaunt's death in 1399. Returning to England that same year, ostensibly to claim the Duchy of Lancaster, Bolingbroke forced Richard II's abdication and seized the throne.

Henry's reign was not a success. He was the subject of a number of assassination plots, designed to replace him with Richard II or later Edmund, Earl of March. He then faced revolts by the disgruntled Percy family in 1403, 1405 and 1408. The revolt by Owain Glyndwr, who claimed to be the true Prince of Wales, did not threaten his hold on the throne but was a serious financial drain. The King's failing health after 1406 led to divisions within the government, especially when his son, Prince Henry assumed a leading role in government after 1409. However, a proposal that Henry IV should step down in favour of his son back-fired and allowed the King to reassert his rule during the last two years of his reign.

Henry VI, 1421–71 Born at Windsor, the only son of Henry V and Katharine of Valois. At the age of 9 months he became King of England, by inheritance, and France, under the terms of the Treaty of Troyes. From 1422–37, however, England was ruled collectively by a minority Council made up of loyal and experienced servants of Henry V. The principal figures in the Council were the Protector, the Duke of Gloucester, and Cardinal Beaufort. In France, the King's other uncle, Bedford, acted as Regent according to the wishes of his brother, Henry V.

As a boy and young adolescent Henry appeared intelligent and demonstrated a determination to assert his authority. However, it gradually became clear that his initial early promise was not going to be matched in adulthood. He was inconsistent and capricious in his decision-making. He was also open to influence. Suitors could persuade the King to give them titles, land, offices and other royal favours which, in some cases, descended into localized disputes between opposing parties. Consequently, patronage was carefully controlled by Henry's ministers who limited access to the King.

Henry, however, could not be criticized and attacks were levelled against his ministers instead. The surrender of Maine (1445), the loss of Normandy (1450), and the final loss of Gascony (1453) were all blamed on his evil councillors. In 1455 Henry succumbed to mental illness, probably inherited from his grandfather, Charles VI of France. Thereafter he became a tool in the hands of opposing nobles. Although the nobility gave their loyalty to the King, England slid into civil war. In 1461 Henry VI was deposed and Edward, Earl of March ascended the throne as Edward IV. Restored temporarily to the throne in 1470–71, he was deposed after the battle of Tewkesbury in May 1471, and murdered soon afterwards in the Tower of London.

Sir Henry Percy 'Hotspur', 1364–1403 The eldest son of Henry Percy, 1st Earl of Northumberland, he was nicknamed 'Hotspur' by his Scottish enemies in recognition of his activities on the Anglo–Scottish border. He was captured and held for ransom by Scottish invaders in 1388–89. In 1399 he and his father played a crucial part in helping Henry Bolingbroke to overthrow Richard II. Hotspur received lands and offices in northern England and Wales, but relations with Henry IV deteriorated as their influence over the King waned. Their victory against the Scots at Homildon Hill in Durham in September 1402 contrasted with the royal failure to suppress Glyndwr's rebellion in Wales. Nevertheless, Henry refused to allow Hotspur to ransom the Scottish captives, and he delayed in paying the expenses of Hotspur's border warfare. Hence in 1403 Hotspur and Northumberland decided to depose the King. Hotspur raised a rebellion in Cheshire in July, but Henry IV intercepted him near Shrewsbury on 21 July before he could join forces with his father. In the ensuing battle Hotspur was killed.

Sir Thomas Kyriell, 1406–61 Kyriell was a soldier above all else. Knighted sometime between 1425–27, he spent much of his life in France fighting to defend English possessions. In 1435 he was part of Bedford's retinue. In 1437 he served under Warwick. In 1437 Kyriell, serving alongside Shrewsbury crossed the Somme and burst into Ponthieu, forcing the Burgundians to raise the siege of Crotoy. From 1437–39 he served as Captain of Gournay and Gisors. Whilst Captain of Gisors he became involved in a dispute over the payment of wages to his soldiers. Lord Beaumont subsequently judged that Kyriell had retained the wages of his men unjustly. This did not affect Kyriell's career. From 1439–42 he was Lieutenant of Calais, taking part in peace negotiations with the French.

After a spell back in England Kyriell was sent to Normandy with a relieving army. On 12 April 1450 he was able to take the town of Valognes. However, his army suffered a disastrous defeat at the battle of Formigny three days later and Kyriell himself was taken prisoner. After his release he returned to England and was subsequently elected knight of the shire for Kent in 1455. Kyriell joined the Yorkist opposition in 1460 and fought for them against the Lancastrians at the battle of St Albans in February 1461. The Yorkists were defeated and Kyriell, in charge of King Henry and the Yorkist baggage train, was captured. Brought before Queen Margaret and the young Prince Edward, he was judged guilty of treason and was beheaded.

Sir John Oldcastle, 1378–1417 The Oldcastles were a leading Herefordshire family who were active in county affairs and the Welsh Marches. Sir John Oldcastle was a notable warrior, participated in the Welsh campaigns against Glyndwr and joined the English forces fighting with the Burgundian army at St Cloud in 1411. His reputation was such that he managed to secure Joan de la Pole as his wife. By virtue of that marriage he became Lord Cobham and gained control of extensive estates in Kent, including the impressive new castle at Cooling near Rochester.

Oldcastle's religious beliefs were the cause of his downfall. He owned and read various heretical Lollard manuscripts. Oldcastle's preferences were exposed in 1413. Henry V gave him a chance to recant but Oldcastle refused. He accused the Pope of being the Antichrist. Condemned as a heretic, Oldcastle was dramatically rescued from the Tower of London and went on the run. Hiding on the outskirts of London, he organized a rebellion which was easily discovered and crushed by Henry V. Oldcastle's last years were spent in hiding. In 1417 he was caught at Welshpool, taken to London, and executed.

Henry Percy, Earl of Northumberland, 1341–1408 Son of the 3rd Baron Percy of Alnwick (d. 1368), by the age of 18 he led English troops in France and was a Warden of the Scottish marches two years later. In 1376 he became Marshal of England and was created Earl of Northumberland at Richard II's coronation in 1377. He served Richard in numerous capacities – military, diplomatic, and administrative – but after 1398 he supported the Duke of Hereford, afterwards Henry IV, and took a prominent part in Richard's abdication.

Henry IV's success in gaining the Crown owed much to Northumberland's support, and the Earl remained an important member of the privy council. The Scottish wars in 1400–1403, however, gradually turned the two Percys, father and son, against the King; they complained of inadequate funds and rewards in prosecuting the wars and of being deprived of ransoms for their Scottish prisoners. The Earl made an alliance with the Welsh leader, Owain Glyndwr, raised a large force, and with his brother, the Earl of Worcester, and son, Hotspur, issued a manifesto declaring that Henry IV had acquired his crown by fraud. In the ensuing rebellion, Hotspur was slain at the battle of Shrewsbury on 21 July 1403, and Worcester was captured and beheaded. Northumberland took no part in the battle, having reached the scene too late with his troops. He retired northward but afterwards met the King and repledged his oath of fealty. By February 1405 he was again in league with Owain Glyndwr and other disaffected nobles and the rebellion was given fresh life. In February 1408 Northumberland was defeated and slain at the battle of Bramham Moor.

Richard Plantagenet, Duke of York, 1411–60

York was one of the wealthiest peers of his age. He enjoyed extensive Welsh and Irish estates and an extravagant lifestyle. York was also acutely aware of his status and lineage, and demanded and received major office under Henry VI. He was King's Lieutenant in France from 1436 and Ireland in 1446. His aggressive mentality prompted numerous clashes with other nobles when he felt slighted or undervalued – most notably with the Beaufort family over command in France and payment for services. He did become Protector during Henry VI's periods of incapacity and gradually attracted enough support among his Neville relatives firstly to remove political rivals around the King, and then to challenge Henry VI's right to rule. In 1460 York claimed a superior hereditary right to the Crown, and although acknowledged as heir to Henry VI, his actions prompted Queen Margaret and her allies to renew civil war to defend Lancastrian interests. York was killed at the battle of Wakefield on 31 December 1460 after which his eldest son Edward, Earl of March assumed the Yorkist claim. After his victory at the battle of Towton on 4 March 1461 he assumed the throne as Edward IV.

Chronology

1386	?16 September Henry born at Monmouth Castle.
1399	29 September Deposition of Richard II; Henry of Lancaster assumes throne as Henry IV.
1400	5–8 January Failed conspiracy by Earls of Huntingdon, Kent and Salisbury to murder Henry IV.
	16 September Revolt by Owain Glyndwr breaks out in Wales.
1403	21 July Henry IV defeats Hotspur at battle of Shrewsbury.
1408	19 February Earl of Northumberland defeated and killed at Bramham Moor.
1409	January Collapse of Glyndwr's rebellion.
1413	20 March Death of Henry IV; succeeded by his son as Henry V.
1414	9 January Henry V crushes a rebellion by the Lollard heretic, Sir John Oldcastle.
1415	13 August Henry V invades France.
	22 September Henry V takes port of Harfleur.
	25 October Henry V defeats French at battle of Agincourt.
1416	15 August Franco–Genoese fleet defeated by English in the Seine.
1417	14 December Execution of Sir John Oldcastle for treason in London.
1418	30 July Henry V begins siege of Rouen.
1419	19 January Rouen surrenders.
	10 September Duke of Burgundy murdered at Montereau by supporters of the Dauphin Charles.
1420	21 May Treaty of Troyes between Henry V and Charles VI.
	2 June Marriage of Henry V to Katharine of Valois.

1421	22 March Henry V's brother, Thomas, Duke of Clarence, defeated at Baugé.
	6 October Siege of Meaux begins.
	6 December Henry VI born.
1422	10 May Meaux surrenders.
	31 August Death of Henry V; succeeded by infant son, Henry VI.
	21 October Death of Charles VI; accession of Henry VI under terms of Treaty of Troyes.
	30 October Dauphin Charles assumes title of Charles VII.
1423	17 April Treaty of Amiens between England, Brittany and Burgundy.
1424	17 August English victory at battle of Verneuil.
1425	2 August Le Mans surrenders to the English.
1428	7 October English begin siege of Orléans.
1429	29 April Joan of Arc relieves Orléans and English abandon siege.
	18 June English defeated at battle of Patay.
	17 July Dauphin crowned Charles VII at Rheims.
1430	23 May Joan of Arc captured.
1431	30 May Joan of Arc burnt as a heretic at Rouen.
	16 December Henry VI crowned in Paris.
1435	5 August Congress of Arras begins.
	15 September Death of John, Duke of Bedford.
	21 September Treaty of Arras between Burgundy and France.

1436	13 April French capture Pontoise.
	17 April French recover Paris.
	30 July Burgundy abandons siege of Calais.
1437	3 January Queen Katharine dies.
1439	July Failure of Anglo–French Congress of Calais.
	28 September English make a truce with Burgundy.
1443	30 March John Beaufort, Duke of Somerset appointed Captain-General of France and Gascony.
1445	23 April Henry VI marries Margaret of Anjou.
	22 December Undertaking to surrender Maine.
1448	16 March English surrender Le Mans to French.
1449	24 March English attack Fougères.
1450	15 April English defeated at Formigny.
	12 August French capture Cherbourg; conquest of Normandy complete.
1451	12 June French capture Bordeaux.
	12 August French capture Bayonne.
1452	23 October English recover Bordeaux.
1453	17 July English defeat at Castillon. Final loss of Gascony.

Further Reading

C. T. Allmand, *Henry V* (University of California Press, 1992). An excellent, rounded biography of the King which discusses his life and reign in detail.

C. T. Allmand, *Lancastrian Normandy, 1415–1450 : The History of a Medieval Occupation* (Oxford University Press, 1983). Stimulating study of the English occupation of the Duchy under the Lancastrians.

M. Bennett, *Agincourt 1415* (Osprey Campaign Series, 1991). Provides a concise account of Henry V's heavily outnumbered army at the battle.

A. Curry, *The Battle of Agincourt: Sources and Interpretations* (Boydell & Brewer, 2000). Discusses a range of extracts from original sources relating to the battle.

A. Curry, ed., *Agincourt 1415* (Tempus, 2000). An excellent collection of articles about different aspects of the battle, particularly the role of the longbow.

K. Dockray, *Henry V* (Tempus, 2004). A fascinating biography offering new insights into Henry V's life and career.

P. Earle, *The Life and Times of Henry V* (Weidenfeld & Nicolson, 1972). A short but useful account of his life with interesting illustrations.

R. A. Griffiths, *The Reign of Henry VI: The Exercise of Royal Authority, 1422–1461* (Sutton Publishing, 1998). A comprehensive account of his reign packed full of details.

G. L. Harriss, ed., *Henry V: The Practice of Kingship* (Oxford University Press, 1985). A collection of classic essays offering fascinating insights into key aspects of his monarchy.

K. B. McFarlane, *Lancastrian Kings and Lollard Knights* (Clarendon Press, 1972). Useful analysis of the formation of the Lancastrian dynasty, the relationship between Henry IV and Henry V, and the impact of Lollardy amongst the upper ranks of society.

B. P. Wolffe, *Henry VI* (Yale University Press, 2001). A very readable account of this tragic monarch's reign.

J. H. Wylie & W. T. Waugh, *The Reign of Henry V* (3 vols, Cambridge University Press, 1914–29). A classic account, offering a detailed narrative of the reign.

Picture Credits

Index